VIEW OF THE INTERIOR OF MR. ALCOTT'S SCHOOL-ROOM.

QUARTER CARD OF DISCIPLINE AND STUDIES IN MR. ALCOTT'S SCHOOL FOR THE SPRING TERM CURRENT 1836.

THE TUITION AND DISCIPLINE ARE ADDRESSED IN DUE PROPORTION TO THE THREEFOLD NATURE OF CHILDHOOD.

THE SPIRITUAL FACULTY.

MEANS OF ITS DIRECT CULTURE.

1. Listening to Sacred Readings.
2. Conversations on the GOSPELS.
3. Writing Journals.
4. Self-Analysis and Self-Discipline.
5. Listening to Readings from Works of Genius.
6. Motives to Study and Action.
7. Government of the School.

THE IMAGINATIVE FACULTY.

MEANS OF ITS DIRECT CULTURE.

1. Spelling and Reading.
2. Writing and Sketching from Nature.
3. Picturesque Geography.
4. Writing Journals and Epistles.
5. Illustrating Words.
6. Listening to Readings.
7. Conversation.

THE RATIONAL FACULTY.

MEANS OF ITS DIRECT CULTURE.

1. Defining Words.
2. Analysing Speech.
3. Self-Analysis.
4. Arithmetic.
5. Study of the HUMAN BODY.
6. Reasonings on Conduct.
7. Discipline.

The Subjects of Study and Means of Discipline are disposed through the Week in the following general Order.

TIME.	SUNDAY.	MONDAY.	TUESDAY.	WEDNESDAY.	THURSDAY.	FRIDAY.	SATURDAY.
IX	Sacred READINGS *with* Conversations.	STUDYING Spelling & Defining *and* Writing in *Journals.*	STUDYING Geography *and* Sketching Maps in *Journals.*	STUDYING THE GOSPEL *and* Writing in *Journals.*	STUDYING Parsing Lesson *and* Writing in *Journals.*	PARAPHRASING Text of Readings *and* Writing in *Journals.*	COMPLETING Account *of* Week's Studies in *Journals.*
X XI	Listening *to* Services *at* CHURCH and Reading	SPELLING *with* Illustrative Conversations on the Meaning & Use *of* Words.	RECITATIONS *in* Geography *with* Picturesque Readings *and* Conversations.	READINGS *and* Conversations on SPIRIT as displayed in the Life of CHRIST.	ANALYSING Speech Written and Vocal *on* Tablets *with* Illustrative Conversations.	READINGS *with* Illustrative Conversations on the Sense *of the* Text.	READINGS *from* Works of Genius with Applications *and* Conversations.
		RECREATION ON THE COMMON OR IN THE ANTE-ROOM.					
XII I	BOOKS *from* School Library or	STUDYING Arithmetic *with* Demonstrations in *Journals.*	DRAWING FROM NATURE in Journals *with* Mr. Graeter.	CONVERSATIONS *on the* HUMAN BODY *and its* Culture.	COMPOSING *and* Writing Epistles in *Journals.*	STUDYING Arithmetic *with* Demonstrations in *Journals.*	REVIEW *of Journals* Week's Conduct *and* Studies.
	others	INTERMISSION FOR REFRESHMENT AND RECREATION.					
III IV	*at* Home.	STUDYING *Latin* and Writing in *Journals.*	STUDYING Latin *with* Recitations.	RECREATIONS *and* Duties *At Home.*	STUDYING Latin *with* Recitations.	STUDYING *Latin* and Writing in *Journals.*	RECREATIONS *and* Duties *At Home.*

TEMPLE No. 7, MARCH 1st 1836.

RECORD

OF

MR. ALCOTT'S SCHOOL,

EXEMPLIFYING THE

PRINCIPLES AND METHODS OF
MORAL CULTURE.

THIRD EDITION, REVISED.

BOSTON:
ROBERTS BROTHERS.
1874.

CAMBRIDGE:
PRESS OF JOHN WILSON AND SON.

PREFACE TO THE THIRD EDITION.

THE great interest inspired by Miss Alcott's "Little Men" has led to the inquiry if ever there was or could be a school like Plumfield; and she has proposed the republication of the "Record of a School," which was published thirty-eight years ago, and which suggested some of the scenes described in "Little Men."

In a note that lies before me Miss Alcott says: "The methods of education so successfully tried in the Temple long ago are so kindly welcomed now, — even the very imperfect hints in the story, — that I cannot consent to receive the thanks and commendations due to another.

"Not only is it a duty and a pleasure, but there is a certain fitness in making the childish fiction of the daughter play the grateful part of herald to the wise and beautiful truths of the father, — truths which, for thirty years, have been silently, helpfully living in the hearts and memories of the pupils who never have forgotten the influences of that time and teacher."

In acceding to this proposition, I find myself, however, in the somewhat embarrassing position of seeming to affirm some crude ideas of my own, inevitably mingled with the narrative, and which in thirty-six years have given place to clearer ones. While my maturer age indorses the instinct which led me to set forth so lovingly this actual and most genuine outgrowth of Mr. Alcott's mind, and I believe with him — now as then — that education must be moral, intellectual, and spiritual, as well as physical, from the very beginning of life, I have come to doubt the details of his method of procedure; and I think that he will not disagree with me that Froebel's method of cultivating children through artistic production, in the childish sphere of affection and fancy, is a healthier and more effective way than self-inspection, for at least those years of a child's life before the age of seven.

But while I say this in justice to my own maturer ideas of education, which at the present moment I am very much engaged in propagating, and would embody in institutions, I have a sacred respect for the experiment made by Mr. Alcott. I believe his school was a marked benefit to every child with whom he came into communication; for he was a greater influence, immeasurably, than his specific method. The moral communion effected by his vicarious punishment of himself for their faults was unquestionably deep, in proportion to its genuineness in himself. What I witnessed in his school-room threw for me a new light into the profoundest mysteries that have been consecrated by the Christian symbols; and the study of childhood made there I would not exchange for any thing else I have experienced in life. For I believe it enabled me to understand, as I should not otherwise have done, the depth and scope of that consummate act of earliest education, which we owe to Froebel.

E. P. PEABODY.

CAMBRIDGE, August, 1873.

RECORDER'S PREFACE.

WHEN the author of the following pages began the journal which makes the staple of this book, it was with the idea of collecting more facts than she already had in her recollection wherewith to illustrate some general views which she deems of great importance. Being engaged in teaching an hour or two each day in Mr. Alcott's school, and being led, by her confidence in his general principles, to look with interest upon the details of his instruction, she found that so much of children's minds were brought out upon moral and intellectual subjects *in words*, that she was induced to keep a record by way of verifying to herself and others the principles acted upon.

This record she has received Mr. Alcott's permission to print in this volume. He, indeed, is not without the hope that these slight details, published in connection with a discussion of principles, may lead to a better appreciation of his own views and plans than could be otherwise brought about, excepting, indeed, by the slow process of waiting results in the children's ultimate experience; which method of verification might perhaps leave him, in the interval, without a sufficient number of pupils on whom to exert his influence, or, to speak more accurately, the influence of those great principles of moral culture of which he would fain be the mediator by removing inward and outward obstacles to their full and harmonious development in the individuals committed to his care. The author, therefore, has availed herself of the advantage of bringing this practical and obvious illustration of principles which she has never before seen systematically applied to any school of children under ten years of age, and which she has only, in the course of her own duties, had an opportunity to test on individuals.

For it is well known that even in our cultivated community vague ideas prevail of a truly spiritual education. The most enlightened people rarely think of sending their children to school except to make attainments in this or that branch of intellectual culture; as if any full, complete, and lively intellectual culture could take place without con stant reference, on the part both of teacher and of pupil, to that spiritual nature, a consciousness of which precedes the development of the understanding, and is to outlive and look back on the greatest attainments of natural science, as the child looks back on his picture alphabet from the height of communion with the highest expression of genius in human language.

The author, however, is not going to complain of the want of confidence and co-operation with a teacher, which must flow from such inadequate views. For she has to be grateful, individually, to many who trusted her for many years, when she was almost afraid to trust herself, and never could have done so with any steadiness, unless aided by that generous sympathy which overlooked her fluctuations of spiritual strength, and forgave her mistakes of detail. Besides, she is well aware that the profession of teaching has not deserved more faith than it has obtained, taking it as it has been at least for the last century. It is perhaps not easy to say where, originally, the fault lay. But the fact cannot be denied, that this employment has been too often assumed, on the part of teachers, with avowedly mercenary ends, or at least for secondary purposes; and that, on the part of parents, there has not been an importunate demand for a better spirit where it was wanting, nor always a ready sympathy and appreciation of it where it existed, — not even in a community where the teachers of adults — the clerical profession — have been held up to an almost ideal standard.

This little book makes no high pretensions. It is an address to parents who are often heard to express their want of such principles, and such a plan, as it is even in the author's power to afford. It will perhaps be more useful than if it were a more elaborate performance; for many will take up the record of an actual school, and endeavor to understand its principles and plans, who would shrink from undertaking to master a work professing to sweep, from zenith to nadir, a subject which has its roots and issues in eternity, as this great subject of education certainly has.

E. P. PEABODY

BOSTON, June, 1835.

CONTENTS.

THE

RECORD OF A SCHOOL.

I.

PLANS.

MR. ALCOTT reopened his school in Boston, after four years' interval, September, 1834, at the Masonic Temple.

Conceiving that the objects which meet the senses every day for years must necessarily mold the mind, he chose a spacious room, and ornamented it, not with such furniture as only an upholsterer can appreciate, but with such forms as would address and cultivate the imagination and heart.

In the four corners of the room, therefore, he placed, upon pedestals, busts of Socrates, Shakspeare, Milton, and Scott; and on a table, before the large Gothic window by which the room is lighted, the Image of Silence, "with his finger up, as though he said, Beware." Opposite this window was his own desk, whose front is the arc of a circle. On this he placed a small figure of a child aspiring. Behind was a very large bookcase, with closets below, a black tablet above, and two shelves filled with books. A fine cast of Christ in basso-relievo, fixed into this bookcase, is made to appear to the scholars just over the teacher's head. The bookcase itself is surmounted with a bust of Plato.

On the northern side of the room, opposite the door, was the table of the assistant, with a small figure of Atlas bending under the weight of the world. On a small bookcase behind the assistant's chair were placed figures of a child reading and a child drawing. Some old pictures, one of Harding's portraits, and several maps were hung on the walls.

The desks for the scholars, with conveniences for placing all their books in sight, and with black tablets hung over them, which swing forward when they wish to use them, are placed against the wall round the room, that when in their seats for study no scholar need look at another. On the right hand of Mr. Alcott is a sofa for the accommodation of visitors, and a small table with a pitcher and bowl. Great advantages arise from this room, every part of which speaks the thoughts of Genius. It is a silent reproach upon rudeness.

About twenty children came the first day. They were all under ten years of age, excepting two or three girls. I became his assistant, to teach Latin to such as might desire to learn.

Mr. Alcott sat behind his desk, and the children were placed in chairs in a large arc around him; the chairs so far apart that they could not easily touch each other. He then asked each one separately what idea he or she had of the purpose of coming to school. To learn, was the first answer. To learn what? By pursuing this question, all the common exercises of the school were brought up by the children themselves; and various subjects of arts, science, and philosophy. Still Mr. Alcott intimated that this was not all; and at last some one said, "To behave well;" and in pursuing this expression into its meanings, they at last agreed that they came to learn to feel rightly, to think rightly, and to act rightly. A boy of seven years old suggested that the most important of these three was right action.

Simple as all this seems, it would hardly be believed what an evident exercise it was to the children, to be led of themselves to form and express these conceptions and few steps of reasoning. Every face was eager and interested. From right actions, the conversation naturally led into the means of bringing them out. And the necessity of feeling in earnest, of thinking clearly, and of school discipline, was talked over. School discipline was very carefully considered; both Mr. Alcott's duty, and the children's duties, also various means of producing attention, self-control, perseverance, faithfulness. Among these means, correction was mentioned; and, after a consideration of its nature and issues, they all agreed that it was necessary, and that they preferred Mr. Alcott should correct them rather than leave them in their faults, and that it was his duty to do so. Various punishments were mentioned, and hurting the body was admitted to be necessary and desirable whenever words were found insufficient to command the memory of conscience.

After this conversation, which involved many anecdotes, many supposed cases, and many judgments, Mr.

Alcott read "The Peaches" from Krummacher's Parables, a story which involves the free action of three boys of different characters; and questioned them respecting their opinion of these boys, and the principles on which it was seen by analysis that they acted. Nearly three hours passed away in this conversation and reading; and then they were asked, how long they had been sitting; none of them thought more than an hour. After recess Mr. Alcott heard them read, and, after that, spell. All could read in such a book as Miss Edgeworth's "Frank." Each was then asked what he had learned, and, having told, they were dismissed one by one. The whole effect of the day seemed to be a combination of quieting influences, with an awakening effect upon the heart and mind.

The next day, a conversation somewhat like the former was commenced; and Mr. Alcott showed that he intended to have profound attention. When any one's eyes wandered, he waited to have them return to him, and he required that they should sit very still in their comfortable chairs. The questions, by interesting them very much, aided them in this effort. After recalling the conclusions of the day before, more fables were read. These he paraphrased, interrupting himself continually to enforce what was read, by addressing it particularly to individuals; requiring them now to guess what was coming next, and now to tell what they thought of things said and done. All then read and spelled, and, after recess, were placed in their seats, where each found a ruled blank-book and a lead pencil, with a printed volume, from which they were directed to copy a passage. Only half a dozen could write. He told the rest, even the youngest, to copy the words in printed letters, and this occupied them very diligently until school was done.

Mr. Alcott's mode of teaching the art of writing is the result of a good deal of thought, having grown out of his own experience as a teacher. He early discovered how to obtain a ready command of his pen, without instruction from others; and, having reasoned on the methods which necessity suggested to himself, he has reduced them very happily to their principles, and constructed them into a natural system, whose results are worth noticing in this place.

When children are committed to his charge very young, the first discipline to which he puts them is of the eye, by making them familiar with pictures. The art of Drawing has well been called the art of learning to see; and perhaps no person ever began to learn to draw, without astonishment at finding how imperfectly he had always been seeing. He finds that the most common forms are not only very falsely defined on his sense, but a vast deal that is before the eyes is entirely overlooked. The human mind seems very gradually to descend from its own infinity into the details of the finite; and the senses give but little help when unaided by a practised mind. It has been demonstrated, not only by the acute reasonings of philosophers, but by observations made on persons * who have begun to see

* The Scotch boy Mitchell and Casper Hauser, for instance.

at late periods of life, that the eye sees scarcely any thing but what the mind has suggested beforehand. Yet by a reciprocal influence of the mind and the organ, this "avenue of wisdom" may become very broad. By attention to children's habits, and by exercise, their minds may very early attain great perfection in the use of this organ, than which none is finer of all that are given to us. The phrenologists say it was their first discovery, that persons who had prominent eyes were remarkable for their powers of learning and using language. Now, since all language is founded on imagery, it follows that perfect organs of sight give to the mind vivid impressions of the forms of things, making the language of the individual picturesque and lively; and thus, even without resorting to the theory of Phrenology, the fact of prominent or fine eyes, connected with great powers of language, has an explanation. But without reference to this influence of clear vision upon expression, there can be no doubt of its effect upon thought. The forms of things are God's address to the human soul. They are the first incitements to activity of mind; or, to speak more accurately, they are the first supporters of that activity which is the nature of the mind, and which can only be checked by the soul's being starved of Nature.

It is from considerations of this kind that Mr. Alcott very early presents to children pictured forms of things; and he selects them in the confidence that the general character of these forms will do much toward setting the direction of the current of activity, especially if we attend to and favor those primal sympathies with which Nature seems to wed different minds to different portions of the universe. But the practice of the eye in looking at forms, and that of the hand in imitating them, should be simultaneous. Mr. Alcott thinks the slate and pencil, or the chalk and blackboard, can hardly be given too early. The latter is even better than the former; for children should have free scope, as we find that their first shapings are usually gigantic. And is it not best that they should be so? Miniature, when it appears first in the order of development, seems to be always the effect of checked spirit or some artificial influence.

With such education of the eye, as a preliminary, reading and writing are begun simultaneously; and the former will be very much facilitated, and the latter come to perfection, in a much shorter time than by the usual mode. By copying print, which does not require such a sweep of hand as the script character, a clear image of each letter is gradually fixed in the mind; and while the graceful curves of the script are not attained till afterwards, yet they are attained quite as early as by the common method of beginning with them; and the clearness and distinctness of print is retained in the script, which, from being left to form itself so freely, becomes also characteristic of each individual's particular mind.

When the pages were presented to Mr. Alcott after their first trial, the hieroglyphics were sufficiently unintelligible, it must be confessed. But (and this is another proof of how slowly the mind appreciates the arbitrary and finite) the serious looks of the children, especially of the younger ones, as they exhibited their strange copies, betrayed no misgivings as to the want of resemblance; nor did Mr. Alcott rudely point it out. He took the writing for what it was meant to be; knowing that practice would at once mend the eye and hand, but that criticism would check the desirable courage and self-confidence.

In the course of a few days, tablets were placed at the desk of each child, on which were large forms of the letters; and they were encouraged to imitate them. It soon became a regular arrangement for the children to pass their first school hour at this employment, and to return to it after the recess. After some weeks, they were taught the small script letter, but not to supersede the exercises in printing. Indeed, throughout the whole teaching, Mr. Alcott recommends that this system of printing should be retained (especially in all those written exercises which children are tempted to slight); for it prevents the habit of indistinct writing, by keeping the imagination wonted to the original forms of the letters.

The ultimate and sure result of this plan is a simple, unflourishing chirography, whose great and characteristic merit is intelligibleness; and constant practice in writing the script gradually adds to this merit the grace of beauty. When a child begins on this plan of writing at five years of age, by the time he is seven or eight he has much of the ease of the practised penman, combining considerable rapidity with perfect intelligibleness and a fair degree of beauty. Mr. Alcott has verified this in hundreds of instances, in his own schools, within ten years. There is a vast deal of difference, however, in the improvement of individuals; and the process cannot be hurried. Time will accomplish it, sooner or later, in all instances.

It was soon found that Mr. Alcott, with all his mildness, was very strict. When sitting at their writing, he would not allow the least intercommunication, and every whisper was taken notice of. When they sat in the semicircle around him, they were not only requested to be silent, but to appear attentive to him; and any infringement of the spirit of this rule would arrest his reading, and he would wait, however long it might be, until attention was restored. For some time the acquirement of this habit of stillness and attention was the most prominent object; for it was found that many of the children had very little self-control, very weak attention, very self-indulgent habits. Some had no humility, and defended themselves in the wrong; there was some correction; but still, in every individual instance, it was granted as necessary, not only by the whole school, but it was never given without the assent of the individual himself, and never given in the room. Sometimes — in the pauses of the reading, for instance — the innocent were obliged to suffer with the guilty. Mr. Alcott wished both parties to feel that this was the inevitable consequence of moral evil in this world; and that the good, in proportion to the depth of their principle, feel it to be worth while to share the suffering, in order to bring the guilty to rectitude and moral sensibility.

On these occasions, he conversed with them, and, by a series of questions, led them to come to conclusions for themselves upon moral conduct in various particulars; teaching them how to examine themselves, and to discriminate their animal and spiritual natures, or their outward and inward life, and showing them how the inward molds the outward. They were deeply interested in these conversations, as they would constantly declare; although, at first, those who were oftenest revealing to themselves and others their hitherto unrecognized weaknesses and faults were so deeply mortified that it was often painful. The youngest scholars were as much interested as the oldest; and, although it was necessary to explain language to them rather more, it was found less necessary to reason on moral subjects. They did not so often inquire the history of an idea or feeling; but they analyzed the feelings which prompt action better. It was very striking to see how much nearer the kingdom of heaven (if by this expression is meant the felt authority of moral principles) were the little children than were those who had begun to pride themselves on knowing something. We could not but often remark to each other, how unworthy the name of knowledge was that superficial acquirement which has nothing to do with self-knowledge; and how much more susceptible to the impressions of genius, as well as how much more apprehensive of general truths, were those who had not been hackneyed by a false education.

A great deal of time was given to explaining the philosophy of Expression. They were taught to see that sculpture, painting, and words, were only different modes of expression; and the casts in the room were spoken of, and they were led to explain those that were ideal. Then they were led to consider gestures, and the *rationale* of manners; and were shown that, as the positions and motions of their bodies were produced by the mind, the mind could control them, and that they were responsible for the impressions they conveyed in this way, especially while they were forming their habits, and had not yet become wonted to particular ones. Lastly, they were led to consider how words body forth thoughts, signing external objects, and suggesting internal facts of the spirit. External fact was discriminated from internal truth, and the youngest children were exercised on such questions as these: Is *love* in the mind, or out of the mind? Is *size* in the mind, or out of the mind? Is *a book* in the mind, or out of the mind? Is *a table* in the mind, or out of the mind? They soon were able to answer, and seldom made a mistake, especially the younger ones.

One great means, however, of making this subject thoroughly understood was by reading to them, and fastening their attention, and then bringing them to attend to the fact of having been thus chained to their chairs by thoughts and feelings in their own minds, which words had waked up. As Mr. Alcott read, his eyes sought all their faces; a wandering mind was immediately detected, and its sign pointed out; and he required them, at any moment that he chose to stop, to repeat what he had last said in their own language, to describe the picture he was calling up, or to give the meaning of the allegory. And as the matter was intensely interesting, taken from the master-works of genius, he succeeded in gaining attention, and also its outward signs. They were soon able to catch the meaning of emblems, so as to preclude the necessity of explanations; indeed, from the first, explanations were elicited from themselves, and not given dogmatically.

"Emblems" (to quote Mr. Alcott's own words in a letter to myself) "I have found to be extremely attractive and instructive to children. I could not teach without them. My own mind would suffer, were it not nurtured upon ideas in this form; and spiritual instruction is best imparted by these means. The universal spirit flows into man and nature through these media; and sense and imagination are the faculties that receive the divine stream, — the one from without, and the other from within, — and pour it upon the soul. The manner of Jesus and of Plato is authority, were any needed, to show what the mind requires in order to be quickened and renewed. 'Without a parable spake he not unto them.' Neither should the teacher of spiritual truth nowadays. By neglecting this mode of instruction, we have shorn the young mind of its beams. We have made it prosaic, literal, worldly. We have stripped Truth naked, instead of allowing her to clothe herself with the beautiful associations in which she presents herself in infancy and childhood."

It was in pursuance of these ideas that Mr. Alcott took so much pains at first to bring out clearly in the children's consciousness a conception of the spiritual world, as alone having permanence and reality, notwithstanding its invisibleness. And when he read, he constantly asked questions calculated to keep attention on the ideas in the author's mind, that were clothed with imagery, or signed by words. So successful was he in fixing attention on the spiritual part of any matter, that not only the imagery of poetry, but every incident of a narrative, was listened to with an air of thought and investigation not always seen in adult hearers of reading.

Their own reading lessons were also made subservient to this object. Thus, in reading in "Frank" the passage beginning, "There was one part of a winter's evening which Frank liked particularly," Mr. Alcott called on each one to describe the room, as it pictured itself out in his thoughts; asking questions about the curtains, chairs, tables, situations of persons in the rooms, &c. Each had a distinct and differing picture from the rest.

It is plain that not a great deal of ground can be passed over; but the effect is to make the reading very expressive, by keeping the author's mind constantly before the readers, and interesting them in his thoughts. There is no greater illusion than the common idea of the method of learning to read by pronouncing pages of matter, which is not moving the heart and mind of the reader.

In teaching reading, in the first instance, Mr. Alcott's method has also been much misunderstood; and, because he thinks a child should never be hurried into or over the mechanical part of the process, some imagine that he does not think it important for children to learn to read at all! It will probably, however, be difficult to find children who know so well how to use a book when they are eight years old as those who have been taught on his method, which never allows a single step to be taken, in any stage of the process, without a great deal of thinking on the part of the child. Perhaps a general adoption of Mr. Alcott's ideas on this subject would lead to some check upon the habits of superficial reading, which do so much to counterbalance all the advantages arising from our profusion of books.

It is a common remark, that the age of much reading is not an age of creative power. Yet why should it not be? Would the mind cease its own appropriate action, if fed with proper food, in the proper way? Can we doubt that there is some error in the general method of acquirement, when it is accompanied by a growing inaction of the creative, that is, the highest faculties of the soul? Mr. Alcott thinks that every book read should be an event to a child; and all his plans of teaching keep steadily in view the object of making books live, breathe, and speak; and he considers the glib reading which we hear in some schools as a preventive rather than as an aid to his purposes. He has himself no doubt as to the ultimate result, not only upon the intellectual powers, but upon the very enunciation of the words, which cannot fail to borrow energy and life from the thoughts and feelings they awaken within the soul of the reader.

But the best reading which children can do for themselves, in the early stages of their education, cannot supersede the necessity of the teacher's reading a great deal to them; because it is desirable that they should early be put in possession of the thoughts of genius, and made to sympathize in the feelings inspired by their master-works, as well as have their taste formed on the highest models.

This is the more important, because our children's books are not often works of genius. In one of Mr. Alcott's letters, from which I have already quoted, he also says, "It would not be easy to form a library suited to the wants of the young from modern works. We have few, very few, that nurture the spiritual life. A dozen volumes perhaps would include all that are of a quickening and sustaining power. On subjects of mere fancy or of fact we have many; but these, if read exclusively, too often dissipate the minds of the young, and materialize their spirits. I have been seeking suitable works for these last ten years, and my library is still scanty; yet within this period hundreds of volumes have been contributed to our juvenile literature.

"Modern works, indeed, whether for children or adults, are too often wanting both in depth and purity of sentiment. Seldom do they contain original or striking views of life and of human institutions. There is dearth of thought and sterility of sentiment among us. Literature, art, philosophy, life, are devoid of freshness, ideality, verity, and spirit.

"The works of ancient writers of a more vivid and spiritual character, are seldom to be found in our bookstores.

"In truth, we have fallen so far below the high standard of those authors, both in thought and style, that we fail to appreciate their beauties of language, their richness and profoundness of thought, their delicacy and humanity of sentiment. How affluent are those deep-thoughted minds! How full of wisdom and love! Their thoughts flow from the heart,—clear, strong, quickening, effective! Open any of these works, and you are upon a deep, rich, fresh thought, clad in imagery, all aglow with life; you feel yourself at once in communion with a great spirit; your spiritual faculties are quickening into being, and asserting their prerogative of insight. You are charmed into reflection. Since the days of Milton, there are few writers whose works require a serene and thoughtful spirit in order to be understood. We seek in vain for depth, freshness; the meaning is on the surface; the charm, if there be any, is no deeper than the fancy; the imagination is not called into life; the thoughts are carried creepingly along the earth, and often lost amid the low and uncleanly things of sense and custom.

"In the discharge of my duties as teacher, therefore,

I have found few books to aid me. I have been thrown on my own resources, collecting from circumstances, or creating from the ideal of my own mind, the material for the spiritual nurture of children. Of the few works that have become established favorites with my scholars, the Bible, 'Pilgrim's Progress,' 'The Fairy Queen,' Krummacher's Parables, 'The Story without an End,' Miss Edgeworth's Stories, are most attractive.

"It is from such books that I read oftenest to children; for Imagination is the soul's shaping power, and, when rightly nurtured, it clothes the spirit in the robes of truth. If there be any fact settled by the history of our race, it is that Imagination has been the leading light to mankind. What, indeed, is Genius but this faculty in its liveliest activity? And Genius has shaped the institutions of society in all past ages. We need schools not alone for the inculcation of knowledge, but for the development of Genius, — the creative attribute of Spirit. And no instruction deserves the name that does not quicken this, — its essential life, — and fit it for representation in literature, art, or philosophy."

"Pilgrim's Progress," read with many omissions and some paraphrase of the text, was for the first three months the greatest favorite in this school. The Bible was the next favorite. In March, the test being put, it was found that the scholars were less willing to give up readings in the Bible than any thing else. The readings in the Bible were not confined to particular seasons, but were called to meet the occasions of the moment, as was Krummacher, which was taken up whenever the influence of his beautiful spirit was needed to illustrate the subject of thought on hand. Mr. Alcott also read to them the Allegory of the Cave from Plato's Republic, which they themselves explained, and which they admired very much; and the death of Socrates from the Phædo, which called forth their tears, and was only second in effect to the story of the Crucifixion, whose life-enkindling sublimity absorbed even its pathos.

But I am anticipating results. The spiritual eye, once shut, is not immediately opened. At first we had some trouble with the older scholars, who affected to laugh at the simplicity of the incidents in Krummacher; but when they found afterwards that they had included, unawares, some of the standard works of literature in what they called Mr. Alcott's "baby stories," they were shamed into silence, and their next step was to endeavor to interest themselves as much as they could, in the spiritual things, that, in spite of themselves, became more and more attractive.

The first two months were given up almost entirely to this preliminary discipline. Two hours and a half every day were divided between the readings and conversations on conduct, and the comparative importance of things within and without. The government was decided and clear from the first, but was not hurried beyond the comprehension of the children; for Mr. Alcott is so thoroughly convinced that all effectual government must be self-government, that he much prefers that all the operations of school should obviously stand still than that they should apparently go on while really standing still or going back in any individual instance. If it should be objected to this principle, that the good are here made to wait upon the bad, it may be answered, that the good are learning the divinest part of human action, when they are taught to wait upon the bad for their improvement; and that there are seldom such actual discrepancies in children of but a few years of age as that any harm can result to the best from being brought to the contemplation of the worst, especially when the worst, as in every case in this school, express themselves sincerely desirous of becoming better, and not one is so bad as not to have been able to ask for correction at some gracious season.

One thing, however, should be remarked as a caution to young teachers. It will be seen in the subsequent Journal that Mr. Alcott is very autocratic. But it must be remembered that this is dangerous ground for a young or rather for an inexperienced teacher to take. It is not, in this instance, taken by an inexperienced teacher. Mr. Alcott has taught school for twelve years. During the first several years, he felt himself hardly any thing but a learner on this sacred ground. He did not, for many years, enforce authority in any instance, unless it was sanctioned by the unanimous voice of a school, sometimes of a school of a hundred pupils. So reverent was he of the voice of nature, that he chose to hear all its varying tones before he ventured to feel that he sufficiently understood what he was dealing with to raise his voice above theirs, in confidence of harmonizing them. Mr. Alcott's autocracy, therefore, is not derivative, but original. It is drawn from experience and observation; and I should add, it continually takes counsel from its sources. And is not this a legitimate autocracy, in the moral sense of the word? Are not the laws of human nature sufficiently intelligible to enable sensibility, observation, and years of experience, to construct a system whose general principles need not be reviewed in every instance of application to every scholar? It is true that every scholar may afford new phenomena; and that the teacher who does not observe these as materials of thought, in private review of the principles on which he acts, thereby to enlarge them, or to rectify such small errors of application as the wisest may fall into, omits the best means of perfecting himself and his art. Besides, a teacher never should forget that the mind he is directing may be on a larger scale than his own; that its sensibilities may be deeper, tenderer, wider; that its imagination may be swifter; that its intellectual power of proportioning and reasoning may be more powerful; and he should ever have the humility to feel himself at times in the place of a child, and the magnanimity to teach him how to defend himself against his own (*i.e.* the teacher's) influence. By such humility, he will also be in the best road towards that deeply felt self-reliance which is founded on sober self-estimation, although entirely removed from vanity.

Before dismissing the subject of Discipline, I will attempt, however, to explain Mr. Alcott's ideas upon punishment, rather more at large than by the occasional hints on the subject, scattered up and down the Journal, since there are some mistakes prevalent concerning his views.

When he first began to teach school, he thought no punishment was desirable, and spent much time in reasoning. But, besides that this consumed a great deal of time that might have been better spent, he was convinced, in the course of his observations, that the passions of the soul could not in all cases be met by an address to the understanding, and only were diverted, not conquered, by being reasoned with. What would excite feeling, he found must be brought to bear upon wrong-feeling, when that actually existed, and to rouse sensibility when there was a deficiency.

Deeper observations of life and of human nature convinced him that the ministry of pain was God's great means of developing strength and elevation of character; and that children should early understand this, that they might accept it as a moral blessing. He, therefore, introduced punishment by name, and found that, in theorizing on the subject with his scholars, there was a general feeling of its desirableness and necessity; and he never failed in obtaining their consent to it as a general principle. On some occasions, there was to be corporeal correction, to consist of one blow with a ferule upon the palm of the hand, more or less severe according to the age and necessities of the pupil. When this was administered, it was always to be accompanied with conversation, and given in the anteroom; though he made an exception once, when one of the oldest boys wantonly disobeyed, for the purpose of displaying to his companions his daring spirit, and needed the mortification of seeing himself humbled before the rest. To the credit of the children, it must be granted that they received this kind of correction without deserting the general principle which they acknowledged at the beginning, and with constant acknowledgment of Mr. Alcott's justice and good-will towards them. They considered it much less severe than to be sent into the anteroom when he was reading.

One morning, when he was opening "Pilgrim's Progress" to read, he said that those who had whispered or broken any rule since they came into school might rise to be corrected. About a dozen rose. He told them they might go into the anteroom, and stay there while he was reading. They did so. The reading was very interesting, though it had been read before; for every new reading brings new associations and peculiar conversation. Those in the anteroom could hear the occasional bursts of feeling which the reading and conversation elicited. A lady who was present went out just before the reading closed, and found those who had been sent out sitting, looking very disconsolate and perfectly quiet, though no directions had been given to them. She expressed her regret at their losing the interesting reading. Oh, yes, we know! said they; we have heard them shout. Nothing is so interesting as "Pilgrim's Progress" and the conversations, said one. We would rather have been punished any other way said another. When they were called in, they said the same thing to Mr. Alcott. He asked, Why? Because the blow would have been over in a minute, said one boy. But this conversation can never be, another time, said another.

Having brought the whole school to this state of feeling, Mr. Alcott introduced a new mode. He talked with them; and having again adverted to the necessity of pain, in a general point of view, and brought them to acknowledge the uses of this hurting of the body (as he always phrased it) in concentrating attention, &c., he said that he should have it administered upon his own hand for a time, instead of theirs, but that the guilty person must do it. They declared that they would never do it. They said they preferred being punished themselves. But he determined that they should not escape the pain and the shame of administering the stroke upon him, except by being themselves blameless.

On the morning this was announced, which was the 1st of March, there was a profound stillness. Boys who had never been affected before, and to whom bodily punishment was a very small affair, as far as its pain was concerned, were completely sobered. There was a more complete silence, attention, and obedience than there had ever been. And the only exceptions, which were experiments, were rigidly noticed. Mr. Alcott, in two instances, took boys into the anteroom to do it. They were very unwilling, and at first they did it lightly. He then asked them if they thought that they deserved no more punishment than that. And so they were obliged to give it hard; but it was not without tears, which they never had shed when punished themselves. This is the most complete punishment that a master ever invented, was the observation of one of the boys at home; Mr. Alcott has secured obedience now; there is not a boy in school but what would a great deal rather be punished himself than punish him.

It must be observed, however, that the point of view in which this punishment is presented to the minds of children is not to satisfy the claims of any inexorable law, but to give a pain which may awaken a solemn attention, and touch the heart to love and generosity. The children do not feel that they escape punishment; for it is taken for granted that they feel a greater pain in seeing others suffer than they would in suffering themselves. But its great object is to display to them that Mr. Alcott's infliction of punishment is not want of feeling for their bodies, but a deeper and intense interest in their souls.

And this was completely effected. A new sense of the worth and importance of that for which *he* was willing to suffer pain seemed to spring up all around, while the unquestionable generosity of it was not only understood, but felt to be contagious. One boy of nine years of age, who was one day superintendent, and obliged, in the discharge of his duty, to put on his slate the names of several boys, some of whom seemed to look forward to their correction as a frolic, and one of whom cried for fear, begged so hard to be allowed to receive the strokes himself, that he was allowed to do so; and it had the most gracious effect both on himself and the rest. The real exercise of magnanimity necessarily elevates the one who rises to it, and who is by nature incapable of vanity (the weakness of the selfish), while the spectacle of it works on the dullest and the coldest. Of course such scenes must be rare; but their occurrence even once is enough to spiritualize all the punishments of the school in which such a circumstance happens.

II.

JOURNAL OF THE SCHOOL.

THE Journal was at first suggested as an assistance to the discipline of the school. It was found very useful at the end of the school hours, to recall to the children all that had passed. Some of the individual reproofs are now omitted, as not suited for publication; but a few are retained, to show their style and nature. I here also omit the details of all the lessons, excepting those on the spelling, defining, and reading of English, which were always the first exercises of the morning, and are made more especially subservient to the main objects of the school.

Before beginning the Journal I must, however, premise, in justice both to the school and myself, that, my record being made at the moment, a great deal was omitted. I found it impossible to seize and fix with my pen many of the most beautiful turns and episodes of the conversation, especially as I took part myself, and the various associations of thought in so large a company often produced transitions too abrupt for my tardy pen to follow, and graceful, humorous, and touching turns of thought and expression which could hardly be recorded by the most skilful reporter.

December 29th.—When I arrived at the school-room, just after nine o'clock this morning, I found all the children sitting quietly at their desks, engaged in writing their journals or their spelling lessons. During this time of silent study, Mr. Alcott generally walks about the room, preparing pencils and pens at each seat, and making remarks. For the study of this lesson, an hour is generally appropriated, which gives time for the journalists also to learn it. About a quarter before ten, Mr. Alcott takes the seven younger members of this spelling class, as they cannot use a dictionary very intelligently, and lets them spell the words over to him, and he tells them their meanings. Of this the rest of the class can take advantage, if they choose. All, however, are thrown into one class at ten o'clock, when two concentric semicircles are formed in front of Mr. Alcott's table, and the spelling, defining, and illustration of the words begin. The arrangements are made without words on the part of the scholars. All turn round in their seats quietly, and form a semicircle around Mr. Alcott's desk. Every chair is at a little distance from its neighbor's, of which the size of the room admits, and which is an easy mode of preventing intercommunication. Mr. Alcott shows much judgment in diminishing temptation by his arrangements. And every day, before they turn in their seats, he reminds them that it can be done without noise. It is very desirable to speak to children beforehand in regard to all such things, for they fail in such duties from want of forethought rather than from insensibility to the obligations of duty; and, while they are always grateful for being prevented from doing wrong, they are often depressed by being reproved for it when it is inadvertent.

Thirty words were spelled; and then they were taken up one by one, and not merely defined, but illustrations of all their meanings, literal and imaginative, were given, either by original or remembered sentences, which contained the word in question. This course led often to disquisitions on the subject to which the word was typically applied.

During this lesson on words, which Mr. Alcott considers one of the most important exercises in the school, he requires profound attention from every scholar. A whisper, a movement, a wandering look, arrests him in what he says, and he immediately calls the scholar by name. When he asks a question, every one who can answer it must raise a hand, and he selects one — sometimes he asks every member of the class — to give what is in his mind upon the word. The most general and strict attention is the result.

Lone was the first word defined. Did you ever feel lone, lonely? said Mr. Alcott. Yes. Always, when there was no person present? No. Ever, when there were people present? Yes. This led to the conclusion that loneliness was in the mind, a feeling independent of circumstances, as one could be alone in a crowd; but that feeling could not exist when the soul was conscious of the omnipresent friendship of its Father, as it may always be.

Look was defined. How does the soul look out? said Mr. Alcott. Through the eyes. How does the soul look in? A very little boy said, By the thoughts turning round. A large boy said, The soul looks in with the eyes as well as out. Mr. Alcott said, Is not the soul itself an eye? And what is reflection? Reflection, said a girl twelve years old, seems to imply a looking-glass. Mr. Alcott replied, It is not the best name for the act of mind I was speaking of; there is a better word for this, — thought. One of the little boys asked what was the name of the soul's look upon things. Mr. Alcott said it was commonly named Perception, and added, Perhaps all the shapes we see without pre-exist in the mind, and are perfect, whether the shape without is so or not. He illustrated this by asking them if the man who made the Temple did not have a picture in his mind of the Temple before it was made, &c.

Meek was defined, and Mr. Alcott described a meek character, and asked if there were any meek ones in school, and whether they knew who these were; but they need not say. Let each one think for himself whether he is meek. One boy said, If I thought I was meek, I would not say so, lest the other boys should say I was proud. He passed on, and they defined more words, which were talked over in the same way.

Then there was recess half an hour. And after recess I took my Latin scholars into the anteroom; and Mr. Alcott heard the rest read in "Frank," and parse English.*

* The details of the more scholastic exercises are omitted, because they would not be interesting to the reader. But it is hoped that it will be observed that these exercises take up at least two hours every day.

December 30th.— When I came to school, I found all the children in their seats, at their lessons. Mr. Alcott, who was walking round as usual, was saying to one of the journalists: You are engaged in recording what happens out of you; its advantage is to make you feel and remember what effect all outward events, and your action on what is outward, may have on your inward state of mind. You write down the picture made by your mind on things. I hope you will soon write the thoughts and feelings that come up from your soul about these things. These thoughts and feelings are your inward life. Do you understand what I mean by this assertion,— the spiritual world is the inward life of all things? All the journalists were looking at him as he asked this question; and replied very animatedly, Yes, and then turned back to their writing.

While attending to the smaller division to-day, Mr. Alcott was once or twice interrupted by the speaking in a whisper of some of the girls, and by one of the boys making a noise with his book; he spoke to them to show them that they interfered by this thoughtlessness with his hearing the lesson, and he contrasted their noisy movement with his own quiet ones in making his arrangements. Mr. Alcott requires profound quietness in school. He thinks that children are morally benefited by being obliged to exercise such constant self-control; and he presents to them this as a motive not less frequently than the convenience of others. In giving to the smaller division instruction upon the spelling lesson, he showed to them how the words might be pronounced wrong, and spelled wrong, and thus fixed their attention upon the precise letters used, and their sounds in each particular instance.

When it was ten o'clock, Mr. Alcott observed that the hour for spelling had come, but that they could not turn round quietly without thought. They turned very quietly. Remarks were made to some boys, because they had made a noise with their books; he said it could be avoided by arrangement. He illustrated the subject by referring to what was a good machine. A perfect machine, he said, was one which made the least noise. Every wheel moved so as not to interfere with the other parts, in a perfect machine. When the machine of this school was perfect, every wheel, that is, every boy and girl, would move without jarring against any other. Two boys said they were not wheels, they were sure; and one added that he did not know what Mr. Alcott meant. Mr. Alcott, who doubted his ingenuousness, expressed surprise at his want of imagination, but very carefully explained his figurative language. All the rest seemed to understand.

He asked if anybody would want any thing during the hour of recitation. One boy asked for some water to drink, but soon after acknowledged that he did not need any, and he would not take it when told that he might. Mr. Alcott had suggested that when one boy went for water, it excited the desire in several others; this, perhaps, led him to feel that it was wrong to ask for it. Some of the younger boys asked to go out, and were allowed to do so; and Mr. Alcott waited for them to return, making remarks all the time. He then pronounced the words, which were all spelled right; and, to illustrate the definitions, he gave the meanings, and asked them to guess what the words were. Some considerations were thus brought up in regard to words nearly synonymous, and the discriminations between them.

A good deal was said about the word *nice*, which was decided as meaning attention to small things. The word *node* was referred to its Latin original; and the figure, by which the intersection of the moon's orbit with the earth's is called a node, was explained.

The word *none* was referred to its origin in the words *no-one*. Mr. Alcott asked them if they could think of nothing at all, or if they did not think of some or one in order to be able to get the abstract idea of nothing. I do not remember this metaphysical disquisition, which, of course, consisted of questions, intended to give them a realizing sense of their not understanding unity, and which probably conveyed nothing more. Mr. Alcott thinks it wise to let the children learn the limits of the understanding by occasionally feeling them.

Afterwards Mr. Alcott remarked that when they obtained one thought, they possessed more than a person who had earned many thousand dollars. The oldest boy said he thought five thousand dollars was better than a thought. Another boy said that he should rather have five thousand dollars than all the thoughts he had had this last hour. Mr. Alcott said, Here is a boy that prefers five thousand dollars to his mind. The boy replied that he did not do that, but only to the thoughts of this last hour. Mr. Alcott said that the thoughts even of this hour were mind. The boy replied that the thoughts of the last hour were not all his mind. Mr. Alcott said that was very true, and possibly he had thought no thoughts in the last hour; but he was going on the supposition that he had had thoughts, when he said that the last hour was worth more to him than five thousand dollars. One boy said he should prefer five thousand dollars to the thoughts of this last hour, even if he had had any. Mr. Alcott said it was very often the case that the desire for the latter interfered with that of the former; Jesus had said it was easier for a camel to go through the eye of a needle than for a rich man to be a Christian, which, in those times, involved giving up his riches, and putting them in a common stock. One boy said he wanted money for his relations. There was a good deal of conversation on this subject; and as it closed, Mr. Alcott asked them if they were sorry to hear such kind of conversation. If any of them did not like it, he wished they would hold up their hands. No one held up his hands.

The word *pall* led to the consideration of the source of palling. It was because the soul was not alive and active. The other meanings of the word were also told.

The word *palm* led to the consideration of palmistry and its absurdity; and to an inquiry into the true sources of knowledge, which opened out an interesting field of remark.

The word *pain* led to a consideration of the uses of pain. He spoke of Pain as a good angel with a mask.

The word *pang* first led to a consideration of the word *sensation;* for it was defined a sudden sensation, and sensation, the boy said, was a feeling. Then one said, A pang is a sudden sensation of pain. Another said, Two boys were swimming, one had a sudden pang of the cramp. Another said, When a master says he is going to keep me after school, I feel a pang. It was thought that pang did not refer to bodily pain so often as to mental, and especially to moral pains. One boy said that men felt pangs when they were turned out of heaven. Mr. Alcott asked him if he thought God turned people out of heaven. A little girl said, that was a pang that came when one told a lie. A boy said a murderer felt a pang. Mr. Alcott then returned to the turning out of heaven, and said, Whenever you are angry, you turn yourself out of heaven. The boy said he did not mean heaven in that sense. Mr. Alcott asked him if heaven was a place, and God sitting there, tumbling people out of heaven: is that the picture in your mind? All the boys seemed to feel the absurdity of this. Mr. Alcott said, Wicked things turn the soul out of heaven, for heaven is a state.

While talking of this, he interrupted himself and said, But you are tired of this conversation: they all burst forth that they were not. Show it to me, then, by your attentive looks, said he; and he went on, and told a short story which had the word *pelt* in it, in order to illustrate the word. The story was of a boy stealing apples. The three oldest boys seemed to think they should have done as the boy did, because they thought the stealing showed the boy's courage and spirit. And his impudence to an old man in the story seemed to be more admirable still in their eyes; and they said they would not have acknowledged the fault and asked pardon. Mr. Alcott made some remarks to lead them to think that it was really magnanimous to ask pardon when in the wrong. But they did not acknowledge themselves convinced.

After recess, I took my Latin scholars into the other room, and Mr. Alcott heard the others read and parse, and gave them arithmetic lessons.

January 1, 1835. — I arrived a few minutes past nine, and found most of the children at the school. There were many exclamations as the children entered, one by one, of "Happy new year!" which Mr. Alcott allowed, although it is generally the rule that not a word should be spoken.

The older scholars were writing their journals, and the younger the words of the spelling lessons.

As Mr. Alcott was walking round, mending the pens and preparing the pencils, he talked to the children, as he passed them, about the difference between happiness and pleasure, and the sources of happiness.

Having suggested the grammatical exercise to the elder scholars, as a means of filling up the hour if they should learn their lesson in spelling and defining before he was ready to hear it, Mr. Alcott attended to the division of the class before him. First, he pronounced all the words in the lesson, and then each of the class pronounced them. Having done this, he directed their attention to the marks of accent, sound, and quantity over the words, and asked them if they knew what they meant; they said, No. He said he would tell them what they meant. He then described these little marks, and led them to observe their forms, and told them he should ask them to describe them to him another day.

It is very important, in teaching young children, to direct their attention very carefully to things in detail, and to each detail at a separate time, for the synthetic is the first mode of perception; it is an effort for the mind to analyze the *tout-ensemble* of sensation or of thought into the parts. The intuitive act of the mind puts things together. A child not only associates outward things with each other very rapidly, but associates the actual picture with the ideal whole, and merges the boundaries of the finite in the great infinite from which it has lately drawn its being. Other people cannot aid the intuitions of the mind, so much as its analyses and its understanding. In one sense, however, the intuitions of the mind may be aided: they may be helped by sympathy, and by removing all the hindrances of development. But the understanding process can be helped a good deal; and it must be done by directing the attention to details, by directing *the senses*, for (although this is a fact that teachers do not generally advert to) the education of the senses in children is naturally behind that of the higher faculties of the soul. Emotions, feelings, intuitions, come first, and interfere with the perceptions of the external world, by their over-mastering predominance.

At ten o'clock, Mr. Alcott told the rest of the school to turn round, but not until he had remarked that there was a wrong and a right way of doing it. He then told the small division of the class to open their books, and look upon them while he heard the older division spell. He first spelled the words himself and required them to pronounce them, and this led to some remarks upon particular words whose pronounciation is disputed. He required them afterwards to spell the words to him.

After the words were spelled, Mr. Alcott asked those to hold up their hands who had been as attentive as they would have been to a coasting frolic. Some held up their hands, and some did not. He then said that whoever interrupted him while the definitions were talked about, might be deprived of the pleasure of recess, and asked if that was just; they all held up their hands that it was just.

The word *nook* was put out, and defined corner. He then asked if there was a nook in the room, which led to a doubt of the perfect accuracy of this definition. He asked if any one remembered a line of poetry in which the word *nook* occurred, for it was a word oftener used in poetry than in prose. One boy remembered a line. Mr. Alcott asked if they had any nooks in their minds. Some said they had. Mr. Alcott said he was sorry, — that a perfect mind had no nooks, no secret places.

The word *nose* led to a consideration of its uses, and its convenient situation in our own faces, and also in the heads of those animals who need a still more perfect organ for their purposes. There was a long conversation about cultivating the senses, and on the abuse of the senses by cultivating them too much.

The word *note* was referred to its Latin original. Mr. Alcott said he should like to have them give a practical definition of it; he wished they would note him and his instructions. All the derivatives, *notion*, *notice*, *notary*, &c., were considered.

The word *noun* was referred to its Latin original *nomen*. Mr. Alcott defined noun as the name of any object in the mind or out of the mind; as the verbal type of the object of thought, whether existing in or shaped out of the mind; and then he asked each one to tell him what a noun was, and they all gave answers, some of which he corrected, filling up those that were inadequate. He then took up a book, and asked what that was; some said a book, and some said a noun. He said, What! is this book a noun? they replied, No, the word *book* is a noun. He asked if the book was existing in or shaped out of the mind; they replied, Shaped out. He asked if the hour-glass was existing or shaped out; they said, out. He asked how it was with virtue; and they said, In the mind. New year, they said, was both out and in. He then took up "Frank," and read words which they referred to the right classes, whether denoting in or out of the mind.

The word *null* was defined annihilate; but the word *annihilate* was not pronounced right, and it was evidently a mere dictionary definition. Mr. Alcott said null meant void, without force or meaning: some people's words are null; some people's characters appear null. He then spoke of the derivatives *nullify* and *nullification*, but he did not enter into their signification very fully.

It was eleven o'clock, and they began to fidget; Mr. Alcott asked who was tired of explaining these words; and one of the boys held up his hand. Mr. Alcott asked another boy what a word was; he replied, something made out of letters. The next boy said, A word is a thought shaped out by letters. Mr. Alcott replied, Or a feeling; feeling may be denoted by articulate sounds also; as *oh! ah!* &c. Why do you come to school? To learn, said several. Yes, said he, to learn words; to learn to word your thoughts; this is a word shop. What do you come to school for, then? he repeated. To buy words, said one. I said, To word your thoughts. Words, then, are the signs of thoughts. What great things words are! a word has saved a life when spoken at the right time.

The word *park* led to a description of the chase, which afforded many animating pictures. These were the most important words defined.

At twelve o'clock, all the children came in, and found their slates ready; those around Mr. Alcott's table had sums to do from Fowle's Child's Arithmetic. The rest, except the seven oldest, found their slates ready for a grammatical exercise, for which the words were to be found in Frank.

The reading lesson was Pinckney's "Evergreens," in the Commonplace Book.

> When summer's sunny hues adorn
> Sky, forest, hill, and meadow,
> The foliage of the evergreens
> In contrast seems a shadow.
> But when the tints of autumn have
> Their sober reign asserted,
> The landscape that cold shadow shows
> Into a light converted.
> Thus thoughts that frown upon our mirth
> Will smile upon our sorrow;
> And many dark fears of to-day
> Will be bright hopes to-morrow.

Mr. Alcott asked, What is the subject? Evergreens. Whose thoughts are these? Pinckney's. What are evergreens? Plants which are green all the year. Have you seen any, in any house or church, lately? Yes, in the Episcopal churches. Can evergreens be made to mean any thing? There was no answer, and he added: I suppose there is nothing in the external world, but it will suggest to us some thoughts. Before we observe what thoughts Pinckney has on evergreens, let us think what evergreens suggest to us. What do you think they teach you about death? They thought evergreens rather taught about life, and the soul which lasts for ever, than death. Mr. Alcott remarked that neither Mr. Pinckney or the evergreens were here; the question is, how can we get thoughts about the evergreens from his mind? By his words, they said.

There was a noise. Mr. Alcott turned to the boy that made it, and said that the greatest and most powerful things made no noise. Did you ever hear the sun make a noise? There was immediately a profound stillness.

Then the class read the lesson, each one reading the whole; and so did Mr. Alcott. He asked which they liked best, the descriptive or the reflective part? One boy said, the descriptive; the rest, that the reflection at the end was most interesting. He asked if any of them, in looking at outward objects, as Mr. Pinckney did in this instance, were conscious of reflections like these? Some of them thought they were. He asked them where they lived most, — in the outward world, or in the inward world of thought and feeling. Various answers were given; one thought she was growing to live in the inward world more and more every day. Mr. Alcott asked if they knew any one who lived a great deal in the inward world. They said, Yes; and he said he also knew a man who lived a reflective, spiritual, inward life more than almost any other; and yet he seemed to enjoy the outward world more than other persons, who lived in it exclusively; and when he spoke, he gave the most beautiful descriptions of whatever was outward. How was that? It was because his mind was in harmony (and he felt its harmony) with the outward world. They guessed he was speaking of a certain individual whom they named, which led to some anecdotes concerning him. I told them of a remark this individual once made on hearing a lady sing after the interval of a year, when he perceived that his pleasure in hearing music was increased, although the acuteness of his hearing was diminished; and an analogous remark which he made, on seeing a cast of the Venus six years after seeing the original. Both of these remarks were calculated to prove that the improvement of the mind could more than counterbalance the decay of the senses, in giving us the perception of beauty in forms and sounds.

When the reading and conversation were over, Mr. Alcott called on the children to paraphrase the two first verses of this poetry; and to paint out in their minds distinctly the two pictures, of summer evergreens dark in the midst of gorgeousness, and of autumn evergreens bright amid the wintry landscape. He then asked them if they had ever experienced the change of the aspect of a thought under different circumstances. This question required a good deal of illustration and explanation, especially as they are hardly old enough to have experienced much of this change. He afterwards paraphrased the piece himself, but said he had not done it well. He told them they might all turn round and write a paraphrase themselves.

Mr. Alcott then took the class in the Child's Arithmetic, and asked the first boy to read the first question, and answer it, which he did. (All of them had the books, in which there were questions without answers.)

He went round the class, calling on each to read and to answer the questions one after another.

After this lesson, he told these little boys to put down their arithmetics and take their Franks; and then he told those who had been attending to the grammar exercise to turn round in their places and take their Franks also. It was now one o'clock; and many of the children had leave from their parents to go home, and consequently lost this lesson.

He commenced the parsing lesson by making them analyze the first sentence, and put the words into the grammatical clauses, and he put the words down on the blackboard as they suggested. Verbs and participles were classed together under the head of actions. Pronouns were called substitutes; nouns were called objects; prepositions were called relations; adverbs and adjectives were called qualities; adverbs of time were set aside without any name. He explained prepositions thus: He asked what relation a book that he held in his hand had to a bunch of pens on the table. They said *over*. Having asked a dozen such questions, he showed them that they gave prepositions for the answers every time. He then referred to their books, and made them tell what relations the prepositions in the passage before them denoted. He asked them about the word *the*, and, finding they did not know how to class it, it was passed over. The word *cottage* in *cottage-garden* was placed properly among the qualities.

This was the same passage which the larger part of the class had been arranging on their slates while the arithmetic and the reading of poetry had been going on.

After this was over, he asked if any one in school thought he required of them too much self-control. One boy held up his hand, but immediately after he said he was not serious. Mr. Alcott said he should be obliged to have a talk with him, he being the oldest boy in school, and often doing this foolish thing of holding up his hand when he meant nothing. He made several personal observations to individuals to whom he had been obliged to speak, for fidgety movements, &c.; asking them if they understood what he wished of them. His object in this was merely to bring out into their conceptions his wishes, as he supposed there was no intentional, but only thoughtless irregularity.

January 2d:—I arrived at the school-room this morning at nine o'clock, and found some of the children at their journals, and some writing the spelling lesson as usual. But a large proportion of the pupils were tardy. This is unavoidable with such young pupils in mid-winter, especially as the habits of Boston people are not for very early breakfasts. The children seem to come as soon as breakfast is over.

There is one study which is pursued at home; this is Geometry. And I hear the lessons as soon as I arrive in the morning; going to the seat of each one separately, and then explaining the next lesson, for them to learn at home.

One or two children spoke as they came in this morning; and Mr. Alcott sent them out, to come in quietly. He chooses that they shall come into school in perfect silence, and take their lessons without a whisper to one another; and this is generally effected without his being obliged to send any one out. It is very important to the quietness of a school that the children should not begin to play in the morning. If all intercommunication is forbidden until they are fairly interested in their lessons, much trouble is prevented.

During the first hour, Mr. Alcott says as little as possible, that he may not interrupt the study and journals. A boy came in who had been absent some days; and Mr. Alcott said his next neighbor could, without speaking, show him the place. His neighbor said, "He ha'n't got no spelling-book," which of course did not pass without revision by Mr. Alcott. Mr. Alcott then stepped out, remarking, before he went, that he presumed that they would be equally quiet as when he was here. Some were; but about half the school whispered and made signs, or took playthings out of their pockets. One boy left his seat, and was out of it when Mr. Alcott came in, who asked him what he was up for. He acknowledged that he went to ask a question quite extraneous to the school. Some conversation ensued on faithfulness.

At quarter before ten, Mr. Alcott took the smaller division of the class, and heard them pronounce and spell their lesson. As it had some hard words in it, though they were of one syllable, he made them each spell every word. Mr. Alcott was sometimes interrupted by the boys, at their seats, drumming with their pencils; and he stopped and spoke to them. He had some difficulty, too, in hearing some of his class who spoke low, and it took a little longer than usual to hear this division.

At quarter past ten, the class turned in their seats very quietly. Two boys who are deaf were moved next to Mr. Alcott.

Mr. Alcott asked the oldest boy what word should be discussed first; for we should not have time for all. He said "oath." Each scholar gave his own definition, and seemed to confound profane swearing with oaths in a court of justice. A great deal of conversation arose upon the obligation of oaths, and the sin of profane swearing. He asked if any of the boys present ever swore. About a dozen of them held up their hands. After a good deal of talk, and apparently general resolution not to swear any more, there were some remarks upon "idle words." After it was over, he asked those who had been interested in this conversation to hold up their hands; they all agreed that it was very interesting, and hoped they should be influenced by it in future.

After recess I went into the anteroom to give the Latin lesson; while Mr. Alcott gave arithmetic lessons to each of the two younger divisions of the school. After the arithmetic, they took their Franks; and when I came in, I found Mr. Alcott putting down their analysis of a passage in the scale on the blackboard.

January 3d. — As it was Saturday, the day when Mr. Alcott generally reads from the Bible, the spelling lesson was put off until after recess; and they were arranged in their chairs, in two semicircles around him. He then began: —

Do any look forward to the ensuing hour with pleasure? One boy said he did not. You may go and coast. Will any other boy go? Another boy said he would. Mr. Alcott told them they might go; but neither stirred. He told them they might go into the anteroom, which was warm; but neither of them went. And without farther notice of them Mr. Alcott turned to his reading, and asked one of the youngest boys what he was going to read. The Bible, said he. Are there any stories in the Bible? No. What is there? Plain reading. What do I mean by stories? Well, I shall read, and you must endeavor to see in your mind what it is, whether a story or plain reading. "Once there was a man named Elijah"— have any of you heard of him before? They all held up their hands. He continued: the time came when Elijah's turn for leaving the world was come, — see in what a beautiful way the Bible expresses that; and he read: "And it came to pass when the Lord would take Elijah into heaven by a whirlwind," — he made a gesture with his hands describing a spiral ascent.

It is impossible for me to describe how this story was read. Sometimes Mr. Alcott would say over, in modern terms, what was going to be read, and afterwards read the Scripture expression; and sometimes he would read the Scripture expression first, and then give a paraphrase.

While Mr. Alcott was engaged in the conversation, he was interrupted by seeing a boy who was a new scholar make a sign to another. He stopped, and said to him: Three months ago, about twenty children came into this school-room prepared to hear instruction; most were all prepared; so they sat down and listened, and were instructed. A few others came at the same time who were not prepared to listen; who did not seem to understand what they came for; who were even angry and vexed at the means taken to give them some understanding and feeling of what they came for. For a time we had a great deal of trouble with these unprepared pupils. They are improved now, but are not yet quite equal to those who came prepared in the first place. Do you understand how this could be? Perhaps you can understand it, and also this sentence from the Bible, — "To him that hath shall be given, but from him that hath not shall be taken away even that which he hath." Do you understand that? Almost all held up their hands. Yes, said Mr. Alcott, you can easily see that all those who had attention and faith have received knowledge and much improvement; but these benefits could not be given to those who did not have attention and faith to begin with. Do you understand that? I do not, Sir, said one of the little boys. Suppose you should go to your mother when she was speaking to you, said Mr. Alcott, and stop your ears, and say, What, what? would you ever find out what she was saying? No. Well, some boys came here with their fingers in their ears, and how could we make them hear? They all laughed. They came with their eyes closed; I mean the eyes of the — "Mind!" they all exclaimed, interrupting him. I wonder how many have their eyes open now, said Mr. Alcott, looking round. They all held up their hands, and he said, Just so many have their eyes and ears open as have faith in their instructors. Have you any faith in your mother, little boy? The child hesitated, and seemed not to understand. Do you believe she loves you? Yes, said he. Do you think she likes to have you happy? Yes. Do you think she is sorry to have you unhappy? Yes. Do you go to her when you are in trouble, and expect she will make you glad? Yes. Do you go to her when you are glad, and expect she will be glad too? Yes. Do you think she is kind to you? Yes. Do you think she is kind when she punishes you? say, all of you, — do you think your mothers are kind to you when they punish you? They all held up their hands. But are you sure you feel that they are kind when they punish you, — when they give you pain? It may be pain of the mind or pain of the body. Sometimes it is necessary to give pain to the body in order to get at the mind. Is it not better to hurt the body than to let the mind go neglected? They all said, Yes. And I hope, then, that when I shall give pain, whether to your mind or body, you will not lose your faith in me, and think I do not love your mind and body, for I love them both, but the mind most, for it is of more worth; and so I would sometimes hurt the body, rather than not reach the mind, when it is necessary to reach the mind and put thoughts into it.

During this conversation, the new scholar again played; and Mr. Alcott sent him out of the room, saying, if he had been longer in this school, he would not behave so. When he had gone out, Mr. Alcott said, That boy is not a bad boy, but he has not thought; he does not know; his fingers are in his ears, his eyes are shut; he needs this conversation more than any person else in the room, and yet he has not enough to have that given him which he most needs. I have sent him out in order that he may get by thought that which is necessary to enable him to receive what he needs. One opportunity of learning it has been necessary to take away from him.

He went on reading the story of Elijah's sweetening the springs of water. He showed that this might teach us how to begin to change a character; you must change its sources. And he said that was the way he began to educate this school. He did not begin by teaching them to read and study; but he went to the sources; he began by trying to make the feelings and way of thinking, right; he put salt into the spring, — not table salt, but the salt of instruction. They all looked pleased.

He then read the story of the raising of the Shunammite's son, which led to a consideration of the continued life of the soul, — whether in the body or out of the body.

There was a great deal of conversation this morning, which I could not record, its changes were so abrupt.

The reading and conversation took an hour and a half; and the children expressed great astonishment at finding that so much time had passed. Some said it did not seem half an hour. Recess came, and the boy who had been sent out was now kept in, losing his play.

After the recess was over, many interesting words were defined and illustrated; but I must omit this. My hand was too tired to keep pace with it.

At quarter of one, the journals of the scholars were brought up, and Mr. Alcott began to read one girl's journal, which described all she had done in school and at home this last week; — and some of her thoughts. It proved she had altered and improved a good deal since she came to school three months ago. A boy's journal was next read; it was a very pleasant account, and contained some good resolutions of conforming to the rules of the school. Then a part of another journal was read; but Mr. Alcott found a difficulty in making out the writing, it was so carelessly done. This boy was not one who had begun to learn to write in this school.

January 4th, Monday. — I arrived at quarter past nine, and found some of the children; but many had not arrived, thermometer being below zero. They took their journals and spelling lessons.

As it was so cold, Mr. Alcott put aside the usual order of exercises, and arranged the children round the stove to read to them, saying that he had made them as comfortable as he could, and he wished them to forget their bodies. One boy said he could not. Mr.

Alcott replied, We shall see. After I have read what I am going to, I shall ask you what I have been reading about. I shall not tell you; I shall ask you. He then read from Thomson's "Winter," "The Freezing Shepherd," and asked, what was that about? One said, about a man freezing to death in a snow-storm. Another said, about winter. What pictures came up in your minds most vividly? A very little boy said, a cottage of little children crying. And so the rest. Mr. Alcott then began to read the same story again, in a paraphrase, as most of the children seemed not to have taken clear ideas or pictures from the poet's own words. They all expressed, afterwards, how much better it was in the paraphrase. Mr. Alcott then read Thomson's description of coasting and skating, and talked about skating and sliding, and other winter sports.

At half-past ten, I went out into the other room with my Latin class, because it was warmer, and returned after recess, — when there was a long talk about partialities in school, during which one of the boys expressed great dissatisfaction at the fact that there was one girl in school who was never found fault with. No boy or girl suggested that there was any fault in this girl; and many spontaneously expressed that they thought she was much better than they. This boy, however, said that Mr. Alcott thought she was the best person in school; and asked him if he did not. Mr. Alcott replied that he thought she might be better than the boy who was asking him that question. The boy replied that that was not fair, and another boy joined him. Those two boys said they thought they were as good, and that Mr. Alcott ought to think so. The rest of the school laughed at this vain-glorious speech.

I then asked the first boy who spoke if he thought there was no difference in characters, and if it was possible for any person to approve equally of all; if it was not impossible to avoid feeling differently in proportion to the degrees of virtue which different characters exhibited. But the boy seemed so much afraid of saying something which would imply that he was not to be admired equally with this little girl, that he could not reason. He persisted to the end in thinking that any approbation of another scholar, beyond what was bestowed upon himself, was partiality. I asked him what he meant by the word partiality. He said it meant an instructor's liking one scholar better than another. This he thought was the meaning of the word; and, moreover, that an instructor's having this liberty of mind was wrong, whatever was the difference of character in the scholars. What was most remarkable, in all this conversation, was this boy's evident want of self-knowledge, or even of the tendency towards self-knowledge. It never seemed to come into his imagination that he might be less deserving than the little girl, whose faultlessness had exempted her from Mr. Alcott's fault-finding. Indeed, he repeatedly declared that he was quite sure he was as good as she; implying all the time that all those things in himself which have obliged Mr. Alcott, almost every day since he came to school, to speak to him more or less, were

5

not to be considered in judging him. The only thing in all this conversation which seemed to give this boy any pleasure was Mr. Alcott's declaration that perhaps the little girl was not the best scholar in the school. He said that he was contented, if Mr. Alcott did not think she was the best scholar. One would have thought that this little girl was the vainest, most overbearing, proud, arrogant person, by the feeling of dislike which this boy expressed towards her. And yet it was the general opinion that there was not a more gentle, modest, unassuming, disinterested person in the room. What could be the feeling that made him desirous of lowering her in our good opinion? Mr. Alcott suggested that there might be envious feelings in his mind; and ended with saying, that although, in literary acquirements, he was superior to some of those younger than himself in school, in moral advancement he thought him behind almost every one, and especially in self-knowledge.

January 5th. — When I arrived in school this morning, the scholars were in their seats, as it was a few minutes after nine. They were reviewing the spelling lesson that was not recited yesterday, and were told to draw a map that was before them, if they should get through their studying before ten o'clock.

At ten o'clock some change of place was made to make them more comfortable. One boy was still dissatisfied; and Mr. Alcott proposed he should arrange it. But the general impression of the scholars seemed to be that this boy's arrangements were less just and generous than Mr. Alcott's arrangements. When the subject was brought up in this way, almost all of the scholars exhibited a good deal of generous feeling, and of interest that the smallest boys, and those whose seats had been the coldest, should have warm ones. I was glad to see that some who are too often selfish did on this occasion exhibit more generosity and thoughtfulness of others than usual.

The words were spelled, and pronounced, defined, and illustrated. The word *robe* was pursued into its figurative meaning, and the robe of the mind was decided to be thoughts and feelings. The question was asked, how they would clothe their own minds. And one boy answered, with an angel, which many more joined in. This was analyzed to mean that good habits, good thoughts and feelings were the angelic robes. Mr. Alcott modified the original idea, by showing that the mind itself was the angel, and culture put on the robe; and he said that he was helping their minds to enrobe themselves with an appropriate vesture of thoughts, feelings, and habits. There was a good deal of allegorical conversation on this word; which seemed to be very pleasing and instructive to the children.

After recess, the first class in reading were arranged in a semicircle; and all the younger scholars (part in Child's Arithmetic, and part in Colburn's Arithmetic), studied their lessons. The reading class turned to a piece of poetry of Mrs. Sigourney's, and Mr. Alcott proposed to analyze it on the blackboard, in a scale which divided words into the names of objects, actions, qualities, substitutes, and relations.

First, the word *object* was defined as the name of any thing; but Mr. Alcott asked the next for a better definition. And it was decided that whatever was perceived by the senses, or conceived in the mind, were objects. Action was defined as any thing you do, or that was done to you. Qualities were defined as the words that expressed the sorts of actions or objects; substitutes as the words which stand for other words, — signs of signs. Relations were illustrated, not defined.

They then proceeded to analyze the verse —

> Why gaze ye on my hoary hairs,
> Ye children, young and gay?
> Your locks, beneath the blast of cares,
> Will bleach as white as they.

OBJECTS.	ACTIONS.	QUALITIES.	SUBSTITUTES.	RELATIONS.
hairs	gaze	Why	ye	on
children	will bleach	hoary	my	beneath
locks		young	ye	
blast		gay	your	
cares		white	they	

January 6th. — Mr. Alcott began the spelling lesson by asking what was the advantage of defining words. And then he asked what a person was like who had words without any ideas attached. One said a parrot; one, a mocking bird; one, an ape. He then asked what boys and girls thought they had been too neglectful of the meanings of words. Several held up their hands.

I observed that one boy, who, in my opinion, is particularly deficient in appreciating the force and power of words, did not hold up his hand, but sat with a very self-satisfied air. One boy, who did not hold up his hand, was very right in not doing so; for he has a very admirable appreciation of words, for his age.

The word *reel* led to a recollection of what is often seen in the street, and the shaping it out in words, till there was a very sad picture on the mind. Other words were then defined, which led to the conception of some other pictures. Mr. Alcott considers that this is a very important way of illustrating words, when the words will allow of it; and almost every word does.

The word *rest* was talked of in all its meanings, as repose, leaning upon, remaining. I suggested that *restore* might be the origin of the word; and as *restore* came from the Latin word *resto*, to stand again, the word *rest*, when applied to the mind, might mean to get back to that repose of innocence in which it was when first created; when applied to the body, getting back to that unagitated state which is the natural state of matter.

The word *same* seemed confounded, in most of their minds, with the word *similar*. One, however, said the very thing was the same thing; which was as near, perhaps, as it was possible for such inexperienced minds to get to the expression of identity.

When these words and a few others were defined, the whole lesson was spelled, and I was asked to read my Journal; but first Mr. Alcott asked if any one of them thought he knew himself. One boy held up his hand; none of the rest did. Mr. Alcott remarked to this boy, that he thought he knew very little of himself; and then he took down Krummacher, and read —

KNOW THYSELF.

Strephon, a Grecian youth of distinction, said one day to his preceptor: I should like to go to Delphi, to consult the oracle respecting my future destiny. I should then, I think, be able to regulate my life much better, and to choose with greater certainty the path of wisdom. If such be thy notion, replied the preceptor, I will accompany thee.

They proceeded on their way, and arrived at Delphi. With a peculiar feeling of awe, the youth traversed the ground that surrounded the sanctuary. They reached the temple, and seated themselves opposite to it. Strephon observed the inscription over the entrance: "KNOW THYSELF." What mean these words? said he to his preceptor.

They are easily explained, replied the latter. Consider who thou art, and for what purpose thou hast received life. A man should first learn to know himself, before he can fathom the counsels of the Deity.

Who am I then? said the youth. Thou art Strephon, replied his preceptor, the son of the virtuous Agathon. Behold, that essence which thinks within thee, and which is about to learn its fate from the lips of the priest, — that essence is thyself. That invisible spirit is destined to govern thine actions, and to mold thy whole life into one harmonious whole. Thus wilt thou become like the Deity, and contented with thyself; for the man in whom the spirit predominates may be compared to a well-tuned lyre, which produces only melodious tones. But he who is governed by sensual passions and desires is a slave, and base lusts lead him at pleasure into ungodly ways. Whoever, then, is thoroughly sensible of his destination, and examines how far he has advanced towards the goal or deviated from it, — such an one truly knows himself.

The youth made no reply. The preceptor then said, Well! let us now enter the sacred fane. But Strephon replied: No, my dear master, the inscription is enough for me; I am ashamed of my foolish wish, and have too much to do with myself and with the present to concern myself about the future.

Repent not thy journey, said the preceptor; thou hast attained thine aim, and heard the voice of the god. Thou art on the road to wisdom; I am assured of this by thy humility, — the first fruit of self-knowledge.

After recess, the usual lessons were attended to.

January 7th. — Still very cold, yet all but three were present and seated at their lessons by half-past nine. At quarter of ten, Mr. Alcott arranged the children round the stove in a square. When the best arrangement had been made, one boy objected, and said he was cold. Mr. Alcott told him to go into the little room where there was a fire. Mr. Alcott then began to have some conversation with them on the subject of making a great noise here before he came in the morning. (It is very uncommon for Mr. Alcott not to be here before all the scholars.) He told them he once knew of a school of eighty scholars, between the ages of four and sixteen, which went on in perfect order for three days, although the teacher was absent, and he said all the lessons were learned as usual. Mr. Alcott then took Krummacher's Fables, and read the story of Lazarus licked by the dogs, and Zadoc's mercy. When he began, he said he was going to kindle a fire for the mind, which he hoped would make them forget their bodies. They listened most intensely to the story; and, when he had finished, he said, How do you like my fire? They all burst out, I like it! Shall I kindle another? said he. And he read the story of Emily, who did not like winter, because she loved her flower garden. As he described the opening out of Emily's bulb into the flower, he made a running commentary of allegory, reminding them that they were germs. They took up this allegory with great delight. One boy said he thought the germs had already begun to open. When he had finished this beautiful story, he said, How do you like that fire? I think it a very warm one, said several at once. They then asked him for another fire. And he read the story of Caroline and the canary-bird. They all expressed their astonishment when he said it was eleven o'clock, and agreed with him that the fires of the mind were warmer than any other. They then spelled the lesson.

Recess-time had now come, and Mr. Alcott said, It

has been very cold indeed, and uncomfortable, but has been an interesting day, has it not? They all agreed, by acclamation.

During the recess, Mr. Alcott prepared the slates and his own blackboard with the grammatical scale for the scholars under eight years of age.

After they had been seated a few minutes, as there was some buzzing, Mr. Alcott asked all those who had whispered or spoken since they came in to rise up. Almost all did. He told them to go out, and come in again, and do as they ought. And they went out, and some of them came immediately back; others not coming immediately, Mr. Alcott went out and sent them in. When they were seated, he told those who had come in last to go out and come immediately back. When it was all over, Mr. Alcott said ten minutes had been lost.

January 9th. — The scholars were at their spelling lessons and journals this morning, when I arrived. At quarter of ten, Mr. Alcott took the little class of four children, under four years of age, and began to read Frank. He began the first sentence: "There was a little boy whose name was Frank." What was his name? Frank, said they. "He loved his father and mother." Do you? Yes. "He liked to be with them." Do you? Yes.

He went on in this manner, and read the two first sentences, which brought them to the fact that Frank was obedient. He here stopped and asked them questions about being obedient, and told them how Anna

Alcott (who was one of them) made out the night before to get up a resolution to obey when she did not want to. He asked questions, and described the whole process of mind. He personified Resolution; and then he said, Well, now, you must say to Resolution, Resolution! keep me sitting still in this chair while Mr. Alcott is reading. He then read the story about the leaf of the table falling, and they looked very attentive and much delighted.

In reading to little children, Mr. Alcott conveys a vast deal of good. In the first place, he requires from them a distinct effort of self-control, by asking them the question, whether they will make a great effort; then he imagines and shows them how they will be tempted, and prepares them both for the temptation, and to overcome it. Without inviting this co-operation, he cannot be sure, that however interesting is his reading, any fixed attention will be given. With it, the listening becomes a moral exercise; for to govern one's self from the motive of desiring to obey and deserve instruction, is a moral action. Mr. Alcott, however, tries to aid their endeavors, by selecting an interesting story; and as he reads, he constantly asks questions to make them co-operate with him, in the manner mentioned above. The result is active and profound attention.

These children spend their forenoons at the blackboard in drawing letters, of which they have a profusion at their desks, and looking at pictures. Mr. Alcott now and then goes and talks with them concerning these. They are required to be very quiet, and not interrupt the rest of the school; and they succeed by means of these quiet amusements. In the mean while they are very much edified, apparently, by the discipline of the school, which constantly conveys to them the theory of quietness and self-control. They also have slates and pencils to copy the forms of the letters.

While Mr. Alcott reads to them, he sits with his back to the rest of the school; but the room echoes, so that a whisper can be heard. When the lesson is over, he turns and asks, Who whispered? and they stand up, and there is conversation and sometimes correction. This plan has many advantages, the chief of which is the habit of ingenuousness it ensures.

At ten o'clock the smaller division of the class spelled their words; and Mr. Alcott told them the meanings of such words as they did not know, which took a quarter of an hour. Then the rest of the class turned round to attend to their spelling. They had an hour and a quarter for their spelling and journals; and most of them had had some time to copy words from the copperplate cards before them. Mr. Alcott said, before he began, that he trusted the school, with its thirty voices, had made a resolution not to interrupt him with unnecessary words, with improper attitudes, or with laughing. Mr. Alcott then asked if all of them were willing to be punished if they broke that resolution. After some hesitation on the part of a few, they all agreed. One little boy persisted in saying, I cannot tell. Mr. Alcott asked him how he was to find out; and to all his questions he answered, I don't know. As

I had the "Faerie Queene" on my table, I carried to Mr. Alcott the passage of the Legend of St. George which describes Ignaro; and Mr. Alcott read it, to the great delight of all, and asked the little boy afterwards, if now he could tell. The little boy replied with a smile, Yes, sometimes. Mr. Alcott then turned round to the rest and said, Ignorance, with keys which he could not use, is that you? But, if you will come here, I will show you how to use your keys, some of them. I do not know how to use them all myself; but I know how to use some, and I do not intend to let any of them rust as Ignaro's did.

One boy in school (who is a lately entered scholar) asked if that story was true. Mr. Alcott said, There are two sorts of truth, — the truth of what is in the mind, and the truth of what is out of the mind. But there are some boys who do not understand that there are realities *in* the mind; and, when I shape out the realities of the mind by means of outward things that represent them, these boys think it is not true. They cannot believe any truth but the outward truth. Now the inward truth is the first truth; there would never have been a single outward thing, not a thing in the world, no world at all, if God had not had thoughts *in* his mind first. The world existed as a thought in God's mind before a single particle of it existed in such a way as to be seen or heard or felt. He then addressed one boy eight years old: Tell me, when you do any thing outside of you, any thing which others see you do, does it not exist first within your mind? do you not feel it first really existing within your mind? Yes. Well, can any of you tell me of a single thing that you see with your eyes, that did not first exist really within some spirit? One boy said, Did that bust of Shakspeare exist really in a mind, before it existed out of a mind? He was soon convinced that the form of it did exist in the mind of the molder.

In the subsequent spelling lesson, when the word *tale* came up, it elicited a good deal of conversation. It was seen that a tale, a fable, &c., might be the medium of conveying truth. Mr. Alcott went on to show that the things that we see tell us a tale all the time. And he asked what the world was a tale of? After a moment's reflection, several of the children said, of God. Then he asked what the things that happen in the outward world were tales of. It was answered that there was not a thing that happened that had not existed in some mind, — either in God's mind or in some man's mind. He then said, The world is a tale, and life is a tale.

I here asked permission to tell the first tale that I remembered Life to have told me. I began with saying that one reason why I told them this was to show how a story sometimes changed its outward form when it went into a mind, and yet carried all the most important truth into the mind. This story, said I, had an outward truth; it was something which happened in the outward world, and was told to me as it happened; and this was the picture that came into my mind.

I thought I saw a dark sea, and a cloudy, stormy sky,

which looked gloomy. And I saw a ship on the horizon, which came on very fast, faster and smoother than any other ship ever sailed, in a beautiful curved line. As it came near, there was a company of women standing on the deck, two and two, taking hold of hands; and each one had white robes on, which fell over her feet; and every eye was looking up, as if she saw God sitting above the clouds; and their faces were full of joy and love. At last the vessel stopped near a large rock on the shore. I did not see a single sailor, or any anchor,—I never had heard of an anchor; but it seemed to me these women walked off the deck upon the rock, and walked over the rock carefully, looking at their feet, and holding up their robes; and they glided over the frozen snow into a high, dark, deep, evergreen forest; and under the trees they knelt down and worshipped God, though there were no meeting-houses, and not a single dwelling-house; and then they went into the bushes, and took broken pieces of trees, and made little huts, like Indian wigwams, which they went into. This was the picture that rose up in my mind as I was told——

The story of the Pilgrim Fathers! exclaimed several, interrupting me; but what made you think the Pilgrims were women? said one. It was the misunderstanding of a single word, said I; and the reason I thought they were in white robes was because so much was said of their purity; and the reason I thought they were looking up was because I was told that they came to the uncultivated desert to have liberty to worship God;

and the reason I thought they looked happy was because I was told that they loved God, and I knew God was good; and the reason that the whole thing seemed done so quickly was because I did not know about sailors, and managing a ship, and anchors, and such things. But now tell me, do you think I gained most truth or falsehood from that picture? The boy to whom I asked the question, answered that I gained more truth than falsehood. Yes, said I, the truth of the mind. Had I seen the thing as it really was outwardly (the Pilgrim Fathers in seamen's clothes, and looking just like any other men), I should not have taken the idea of how different their minds were from those of common people; for I could not have seen their thoughts. But my imagination shaped out their thoughts in such a way that I could see their very thoughts; and so the very mistakes which I made helped me to see more of the truth than I should have seen, had my real eyes been there, looking at their real bodies. It was of great use to my character to have this picture of true devotion, of souls so full of goodness as not to mind cold, nor the having no homes; and caring so much about worshipping in the way they thought was right, that they were willing to live in that wilderness. Especially since I thought they were women!

Mr. Alcott said, And now see the advantage of having an imagination which is always ready to give the most beautiful shapes to words. It makes a great deal of difference in your characters, whether there are beautiful shapes in your minds or not; and, in using words, you should take great care to use such as may put shapes into the minds of others, which will mold them right. Suppose a man says to a child, You *brat* you, get out of my sight! What an ugly picture the words make in that child's mind of himself! So that he can hardly feel that he has a spirit within him. Well, it is not true that he has a spirit within him, said one boy. Not true! said Mr. Alcott; indeed it *is* true; and until you feel that you have a spirit within you, and must act according to it, you will never be free from those thoughts and feelings and actions that trouble you and us so much every day. If I did not think there was something within you much more angelic than has yet appeared, I should feel very despairing. If I thought of you as you think of yourself, I should be as discouraged as you are. You think you are good enough; but I believe you can be a great deal better.

I thought an angel was a man with wings, said one boy. What do the wings mean? do they mean the feelings that go upward? All men have such wings. Men are not angels, said another boy. I pointed to a picture that hung in the room, and asked if he thought much of what that person thought. He said, Yes. Well, said I, I heard him say once that unless we could believe in the angels that were around us in shapes of men, it would do us no good at all to believe there were angels in another world. He seemed to be quite struck with the force of this person's authority. Mr. Alcott then took Krummacher's Fables, and read, by way of illustrating the subject, —

ADAM AND THE SERAPH.

One evening Adam was reposing on a hill under a tree in the garden of Eden; and his face was turned upward, and his eyes were fixed on heaven. A seraph drew nigh unto him, and said, Why lookest thou up so wistfully towards heaven? What aileth thee, Adam? What should ail me, answered the father of men, in this abode of happiness? My eye was observing the stars which glisten yonder, and I wished for the wings of the eagle, that I might fly up to them, and obtain a near view of their brilliant orbs.

Thou hast such wings, replied the seraph; and he touched Adam, and Adam sank into a deep sleep and dreamt; and it seemed to him in his dream that he was flying up to heaven.

When he afterwards awoke, he looked around him, and was amazed because he was lying under the tree on the hill. But the seraph stood before him, and said, Wherefore musest thou, Adam? Adam answered and said, Behold, I was up yonder in the firmament of heaven, and walked among the stars, and flew around Orion and the Pleiades; brilliant orbs, vast and glorious as the sun, whirled past me,—the milky way, which thou seest yonder, is an expanse full of bright spheres, and above this expanse is another, and again another. And in these shining worlds dwell beings like unto myself; and they pray to the Lord, and praise his name: seraph, didst thou conduct me?

This tree, answered the seraph, hath overshadowed

thee, and thy body hath not quitted this hill. But behold, Adam, within thee dwelleth a seraph, that hath the faculty to traverse the boundless regions of space, in which innumerable spheres revolve, and the higher he ascends the more profound is his adoration of Jehovah. Guard this seraph, Adam, with care and vigilance, that the passions may not obstruct his flight and fetter him to the earth. The seraph spake, and disappeared.

Mr. Alcott asked them if they understood what he intended to teach them by reading this. They replied, Yes.

After recess, I took my Latin class into the other room, and they all had their slates given to them, and began to analyze sentences into the parts of speech, and into the variations of cases. In the mean time, those who were with Mr. Alcott had read in Frank; and he had asked the children what pictures certain words brought up to their minds, and had had several interesting answers. One boy of six said *Try* shaped itself as a strong man. And another of five gave quite an elaborate picture of *Day*. He said he thought of an angel sitting on the floor of heaven, which was our sky, and letting down, through an opening, a cross, in which was the sun. When he lets down the cross, it is day, and, when he draws it up, it is night. He made appropriate gestures as he described this. Where did you get that picture? It came into my mind all of itself. When? Why, now. Did you ever think of that picture before to-day? No. In regard to some other particulars which were asked in order to ascertain if it was distinct and steady before his mind, he answered without hesitation.

Another question which Mr. Alcott asked of the little boys was, how they employed rainy days. They gave various answers; and this boy said that he sat down and thought over the stories he had heard, and acted them over in his mind, and sometimes made up new ones,—oh, very beautiful! with angels in them. This little boy afterwards added an angel of the moon, who sat by the side of the angel of the sun, and, when the sun was drawn up, put down the moon in the same way. This angel also put down the stars, but not in crosses. He hung them down. But in the morning, when the cross of the sun is put down, these stars shoot back into heaven, said he, like balloons.

January 10*th.*—There was some mistake about the fire; and, as the room was very cold, Mr. Alcott took all the children into the anteroom, there to spell and define the lesson, without having previously studied it. They remained with him till half past eleven, conversing upon the interesting subject, Conscience. The question arose, whether it was seated in the head or heart; and it was remarkable that those boys whose conscience is to them the surest guide, and the most powerful, all thought it was in their heart, while those who are not so conscientious thought it was in their head.

In the grammatical analysis to-day, there was some conversation about the word *object*, and it was found by its etymology to mean what lies out of or before the mind. What mind laid things out of itself, — laid out before it every thing? God, said a boy of seven. Did he put any thing into things by which they might get up? Yes, in some things he put spirit, his own spirit. And so all things that have spirit within them get up and act as much as they can? No, said he, laughing; some are sluggards. What are you in earnest about? said Mr. Alcott to the little boy of five, mentioned yesterday. Not about any thing. What is being earnest? Feeling that things must be done. And you do not feel so about any thing? Only about being good. O Mr. Alcott! I have thought of an angel of rain. Well, how does he look? He sits by the angels of the sun and moon. Do they help him? No. How does he know when to have it rain? Oh! he can see; he knows when it is dry down here; and he went on to describe his operations, but I could only understand that the angel took the water in a great bubble from the sea, and went up in it, and came down with the rain.

January 12*th.* — I arrived at a few minutes after nine, and found the children at their lessons. At a quarter of ten, Mr. Alcott took his youngest class, and began with telling over what he had read about in Frank the last time. Mr. Alcott asked them if they minded as Frank did. One held up his hand. Mr. Alcott said, You mind sometimes; well, that is better than not at all! But do you mind when you don't want to? No. Ah! but Frank did; because he thought, and he knew that his mother's wants were better than his own. He then went on, and read in another place about Frank's going over the stile, &c.; and after he had done, he said, Well, now you have heard about meddling; the other day you heard about minding. Do you meddle?

At ten o'clock, he took the youngest division of the spelling class, as usual, and heard them spell, and told them the meanings of the words. This lasted a quarter of an hour, when the rest of the class turned. At first Mr. Alcott spelled the words, and called on the scholars to pronounce them. Then he gave the definitions, and required them to tell the words; then he called for an illustration of each word, in original or quoted sentences, in which the word was used. As usual, this led to a great deal of conversation; for the figurative uses of the words being brought in among the illustrations, Mr. Alcott always pursues the spiritual subjects thus introduced, thinking it the most natural way of interesting their minds in mental operations. Thus the word *steep* being illustrated by the expression, "steeped in wisdom," led to a consideration of the source of wisdom being an inexhaustible fountain. One boy said, with great simplicity, that he was not yet wet through with wisdom.

The word *spot* led to unspotted, — unspotted in character, — Jesus Christ, — the original innocence of character in childhood, — how they had become spotted (by disobeying conscience, not obeying parents who interpret conscience, by getting into passions, loving appetite too well, &c.). These disquisitions are always conversations; the references to Jesus Christ are always by describing his character; they respond saying, I know who you mean, and pointing to the cast of Christ. There is a strong expression of reverence, and natural sensibility to excellence, whenever he is referred to.

One of the words led to a discrimination between the words *character* and *reputation*, and then to a discrimination between the character and nature of a person. In the course of the conversation, the question arose, whether Mr. Alcott understood their characters. Some of the boys said they thought he did; others thought he did not. This led to a consideration of the evil of secretiveness, and the beauty and advantage of transparency. Secretiveness, Mr. Alcott thought, was naturally connected with selfishness, and frankness with generosity.

Mr. Alcott asked if all deserved to go out at recess, when there had been so much noise. One boy said he thought the good ought not to suffer for the bad. Mr. Alcott replied that in God's world the good oftentimes suffered for the bad; and that it was a proof of a person's being good, that he was willing to suffer for the bad. The boy replied that he was very wicked, then, for he was not willing to suffer for the bad.

January 13*th.* — Mr. Alcott read to his youngest class, from Northcote, a story about a dog, which I wish I could describe, with his conversation intermingled, but I cannot.

At ten he took the youngest division of the class, as usual. When the rest of the class turned, Mr. Alcott said, What is a definition? One girl replied, It is the meaning of a word. What is the meaning of a word? The explanation, said another girl. The thought told in other words, said one of the boys. The definition of a word is to tell all its meanings, said another. The meaning of a word, said Mr. Alcott, and the definition are not the same. As you have a soul within your body, and your body means out, as it were, the soul, so the word has a soul. What do you think of such an idea as the soul of a word? Can you take that idea, — the spirit of a word? Yes, sir, said one little girl, very intelligently.

Now, said Mr. Alcott, let us see if we can find the spirits of these words; if we can open the words, and bring out the thoughts and feelings. You have seen a very little seed, a mustard-seed; the meaning of that seed is not seen, till it has opened out into the branches, and leaves, and fruits.

The first illustration of the word *soar* was the figurative one. "Our minds soar when they think on some subjects." He asked if there were any who were conscious that their minds and hearts were beginning to soar. One boy held up his hand. Two other boys expressed a wish that they had the eyes and wings of the eagle. Mr. Alcott said, You have stronger wings than the eagle, and eyes to see a brighter sun than he has ever seen. Mr. Alcott then went very carefully over the process of an egg's being nursed into life; the warmth of the parent bird operating upon the matter around the germ of life, and making it so pliable that the germ of life, which is spirit, shapes out a form that will mean something to the observing mind. He then went over the process of a bird's learning to fly, through the encouraging love and care of the parents, animating the spirit of life, and leading it out. He then asked some questions about their minds soaring out of their bodies; and some interesting answers were given. He then brought forward a cast of a child, whose arms were stretched upwards; and asked each one of them what idea this image awakened in his mind. One boy said, of a boy stretching. But almost all the boys expressed the spiritual idea of aspiration. One boy said it was an angel (yet there were no wings). One girl said it was a soul, shaped out as a child, ascending to a higher state. One boy said it seemed to be a child looking up to heaven, and praying to God to send an angel down to take it up to heaven; and that it was preparing to be received there.

One very intelligent boy, the shape of whose head seems to indicate the possession of the imaginative faculties, and who has expressed strongly the desire of pursuing the fine arts, said he took no idea. Mr. Alcott replied that he did not do justice to himself in saying that. But I said I thought that he would not take pains to clothe his thoughts and feelings in words; or that perhaps he was proud, and did not wish to attempt it, lest he should fail. And yet there was no way for him ever to learn how to express himself, except by attempting it, and being helped out. I wished he would do this, for I felt sure it would bring him a great deal of satisfaction; and, when he had once got over the difficulty, he would not sit, his soul sending the blood out of his heart into his head, and driving it back again into his heart, while he feels overwhelmed with feelings that he does not know how to define. I told him he reminded me of a child that I once knew, who carried this fault of pride so far that he has become a very unhappy man.

Mr. Alcott asked which was most interesting, such conversation as this, or conversation about steam-engines or such things. Many said, such conversation as this; but some did not reply. Mr. Alcott put the qnestion in another form; and at last a little boy exclaimed, I never knew I had a mind till I came to this school; and a great many more burst out with the same idea. I asked a very little boy, who I think has improved in his intellect more perhaps than any other child in this school, if he knew that he had a mind before he came to this school. He said, Yes. I then asked him if he ever thought before. He said, Yes. If he ever thought about his thoughts. He said, with a bright smile, No! If he liked to think about his thoughts. He said, Yes. If he liked it better than to think about any thing else. He said, Yes. If it entertained him. He said, Yes, yes, yes. Mr. Alcott then asked all those who liked to think about their thoughts better than about how things were made and done to hold up their hands; and almost every scholar held up his hand for thoughts.

One boy then said he liked things which represented thoughts. Mr. Alcott said, Yes, that is beautiful; that is a way of studying things which is most interesting. But of course no one can think about things as representing thoughts, until they have first thought about thoughts in themselves. This boy then said he wanted to ask if the mind did not mean that part of us which took in learning, as astronomy, &c., and the soul that part of us which takes in the thoughts of God and duty: Is there not this difference, said he, for I never knew certainly? Mr. Alcott agreed that there was this difference, and told him the word *spirit* included both, and the voice of the spirit was conscience; for both the mind and soul were necessary to inform conscience, and make it express itself perfectly and wisely. Mr. Alcott said that some people seemed to be mostly mind, and some mostly soul; but the union of the two in proper proportion constituted the life of the spirit, and made it utter its voice in conscience.

I then told the history of the mind I referred to above, and how without vanity, but through pride, he kept himself back; how the fear of revealing his wants, even when he intensely felt them, deprived him of all assistance; how he never attempted to do any thing until he was able to do it perfectly; how, at last, he seldom attempted to do any thing at all, because he knew he could not do it perfectly; and how it had all resulted in his powers of action being so very much behind his conceptions of what might and could be done that he did not have any sense of success, became gloomy, and was going on in doing things inferior to his own capacity, without the means of communicating his mind to those in whom alone he felt interest. I ended with saying, There are some persons here who have in a degree the pride and the habit of that person; and I would warn such of the consequences.

As I told this in a very detailed manner, it excited great attention and interest; and several acknowledged that they felt they had a degree of the same spirit. The individual I particularly thought of was particularly conscious; and I had a long conversation with him, in recess, upon the duty of overcoming this pride, and not fighting against his own mind. I stimulated him by giving him instances of persons very superior in the power of expression, and endeavored to show him that they never would have been able to sway the minds of others with the thoughts in their minds, unless they had done differently from the way he was doing; for he was repressing his mind, by putting down his thoughts into the measure of such words as he already possessed, instead of allowing his thoughts and feelings to go forth after expression, as certain other boys did whom I named, who were every day improving. He asked what he could do. I said, Endeavor to answer every question Mr. Alcott puts out, instead of using your mind, as you do now, to evade answering the questions at all; for this will certainly cramp and in the end destroy it. He seemed to understand this argument, and disposed to follow this advice.

After recess, Mr. Alcott took "Pilgrim's Progress," and read the first description of Christian very slowly, and all his distress, and the want of sympathy of those around him, through the interview with the Evangelist, and the Slough of Despond, up to the place where the Interpreter shows Christian the picture. He explained as he read, applying it to the spiritual condition of individuals in the school; and in some instances we had quite a general conversation. When he came to the description of the first picture in the Interpreter's house, he stopped, and asked, why were the eyes looking upward? One girl said, because he was endeavoring to get to heaven. Another said, because he was tired of earthly things. A boy said that the eyes looked upward because he loved God, and was thinking about him. Another boy said, because he had a disposition to go to heaven. Some said they had no thoughts. Mr. Alcott asked one if he thought that Mr. Alcott wished his body to be here without his mind, i. e. without any thoughts. The boy blushed. Mr. Alcott asked, why was it said that "truth was written on his lips"? Many answered, because he looked as if he spoke the truth. They all spoke as if they understood truth as merely veracity. He asked why the world was behind his back. One boy said, because he preferred heaven to earth. Others confined their notion to that of his being tired of the world. Why was the crown suspended over his head? One girl said, to show that he would be rewarded for being good. Another girl said, for his perseverance. A boy said, for loving heaven better than earth. What is this way of representing truth called? Allegory. I have been reading an allegory, which pictures out truth by — what? As they could not get the word, he said emblems, and that they had been interpreting the emblems. Mr. Alcott then went on and read all the things which the Interpreter showed to Christian.

Something was said about our most imaginative boy, who was not present to-day. The scholars delight in hearing his ideas generally; but one who is some years older, and very fond of admiration, has expressed some feelings of jealousy. It was remarked that there was nothing extraordinary in itself in any thing this boy said; that all children have such ideas in their souls, and more beautiful ones too; and that all the difference in the shaping power arises from the habit of looking into himself which this boy has, and some children have not. It is only wonderful in itself that you do not all give us as beautiful thoughts as he does; and it can only be accounted for by remembering that parents and school-teachers have not done what they might have done to keep you from giving yourselves up to bodily pleasures and eye enjoyments, without taking the trouble to think, all the while. Play is an excellent opportunity for exercising your imaginations. But you often push one another about, instead of playing something with a plan. I have known children play long stories, making believe a thousand things; making believe is using your imagination. But you should never make believe bad things. And I knew a boy who made himself hard-hearted, by always playing Indian wars. But I have known some children cultivate their minds and hearts, without knowing it themselves, by their beautiful plays. Some anecdotes were added.

January 14*th*. — I arrived at few minutes after nine, and found the children at their lessons. Mr. Alcott read to his little class the story of Frank's going into the garden. He read as far as why people could not take whatever they wanted; and then there was a good deal of conversation with them on meddling, and on not spoiling other people's things.

At nearly ten, Mr. Alcott took the smallest division of his spelling class, and began with asking one boy, if, when he talked with his father or mother, he ever used any of the words he found in his spelling lessons. He said, Yes. The two next boys said they never used these words. Mr. Alcott said, Suppose I should put a box at your seat with six words in it, which were names of your thoughts, and different names from any you had ever heard of, and you opened your box and said, Well, I do not know what thoughts these words are names of, but Mr. Alcott will tell us; and so Mr. Alcott comes and tells you, and you go home and talk out your thoughts with these new words; you would learn six new words every day. Well, let us look into your spelling lesson, and see if we can find some new names to your thoughts. When he had told them the meanings of the words, he illustrated them by sentences in which they were used figuratively.

During this lesson, he spoke to two girls for whispering; and he remarked that this was the first whisper he had heard since school began, the first time he had had to speak to any scholar for any thing. The little girls looked quite ashamed.

At ten minutes past ten, Mr. Alcott asked the rest to turn in their seats, and expressed his approbation of their stillness, which he thought had been remarkable. He then placed two boys, who were apt to be fidgety, at a distance from the rest, and proceeded to the lesson, saying, This exercise, which we call spelling and defining, leads to a great deal; it not only teaches to spell the words, but to see how thoughts and feelings are expressed by words; it gives names to thoughts and feelings. Now, tell me, what advantages does this lesson lead to? One of the boys repeated his remark, and added, We learn the pronunciation of words also. Another here began to say that he thought he knew the meaning of words before he came to this school; and he seemed to think that he knew so much of words before, he was not very much benefited by this exercise, since only a few words were defined each day, and the illustrations took so long a time.

After satisfying this boy of his error, Mr. Alcott continued his remarks on the spelling lesson; saying that there were nine thousand words in this spelling-book, and that they touched almost every subject of thought, feeling, action, and conduct; and, in going over them, some important ideas on all these subjects might be attained, and they would have acquired the very soul of the language.

The words were all spelled rightly; and as the boys all sat perfectly still, Mr. Alcott said, referring to the circumstance of having appointed a superintendent during this hour, What effect a thought has, — the thought of keeping one's name off a slate! A thought, with a little will in it, keeps all these bodies still. What power a thought has! it is very real, and quite as real as the body it keeps still.

Took was illustrated thus: It took an hour to say the lesson; he was taken; and a story was told that had the word in it several times, and which also had the advantage of inculcating a moral lesson. A good deal was said of its various meanings; and its grammatical distinction from *take* was mentioned.

Tool was illustrated by a wood-saw, a plane, a trowel. The sentence, One person makes a tool of another, introduced a consideration of the depravity which led one person to make a tool of another; the want of comprehension of the sacredness of the human mind, which could allow any one to make it a tool. He illustrated this by stories. He ended with saying, No mind is to be made a tool of, — no, not even by one's self. I know some boys who make their minds the tools of their bodies, and that is very bad.

Among his illustrations of *tool*, he spoke of school-masters who made tools of their scholars wherewith to build up their own fortunes; and he spoke of one school-master who had this plan, and who wanted him to assist him! And he related their conversation, and thus had an opportunity of giving the scholars an idea of his own principles and views in pursuing this vocation. They seemed deeply interested, and I thought it fortunate that he took the opportunity of bringing them to understand what his views were, since it gave them an opportunity of appreciating and co-operating with him; and nothing is more important than for children to have a perception of a sacred sense of duty inspiring the instructor, for reverence is the baptism of soul which is necessary to prepare for "the mysterious communion of ignorance with wisdom."

Parents do not always understand the indispensableness of this baptism, and often do their children a moral injury, which is utterly irreparable during the whole period of youth, by putting them under the care of persons whom they cannot or do not treat with reverence themselves. There is not a procedure more profligate towards the child, to say nothing of the instructor, than for a parent to do this. There is no intellectual advantage (I do not hesitate to say) which can compensate for this moral disadvantage. And the intellectual disadvantage, in a majority of instances, is only second to the moral. For real intellectual action is intimately connected with the proper state of the soul. It can only be continuous, persevering, and honest when its motive is moral. There must be a perfect self-surrender, for the time being, in order that the intellect may see what is before it. Reservation throws a cloud over that which is to be presented to the mind; for to childhood, reservation is always an effort, and in exactly the contrary direction from the effort of taking in ideas. But there will be reservation — there can be no self-surrender — when there is want of faith in the instructor; and this faith is to be inspired by sympathy from parents.

He proceeded to the word *type*. What is a type? said he. One boy said, A type is a metal letter which is used to stamp a sign upon paper. What is a word the sign or type of? said Mr. Alcott. They severally said, of a thought; of an idea; of a feeling; of an object; of an action; of a quality. Language, said Mr. Alcott, is typical of whatever goes on within us, or is shaped out of us. What is the body a type of? Of the mind. What is the earth a type of? Of God, mind, heaven, were the several answers. I would go on much farther, said Mr. Alcott, if there was time. There are people who think and say that the world and outward things are all, because they do not know what they are typical of. I could show you that all outward things are produced out of those spiritual realities of which they are types. But the clock now typifies the hour of recess; and you may go out.

At the hour of dismissal, the whole school was brought together. One or two boys had been punished on their hands during the school hours, and one of the larger boys remarked that a certain gentleman (naming him) had said that he was sorry Mr. Alcott had found it necessary to use the ferule. Mr. Alcott said, Such of you as have been punished with the ferule may rise.

Several did so. He then said, Such of you as have been made better, have been assisted in self-control, and in your memory, by being so punished, may sit down. All sat down but one. Mr. Alcott then remarked that he was sorry thoughts were not realized as they might be, to govern their actions. But as sometimes they were not, and many boys deemed thoughts to be unreal, it was necessary for outward things, which they did believe real, to take the side of conscience, and help to make them seem real and visible; and he believed not one boy had been punished, without acknowledging, beforehand, that he felt it would do him good, and that it was Mr. Alcott's duty to give him that help. There was much conversation, which seemed quite satisfactory all round. Mr. Alcott then said that the gentleman referred to was very wise in his judgment on a case that he knew; but that it was not every boy who knew how to state a case truly, since, in order to state any case truly, it must be seen truly; and it required self-knowledge and self-surrender to see truth in all cases. Was this boy capable of such self-knowledge and self-surrender as to state a case whose circumstances condemned himself? We saw every day that here he could not even see any circumstances just as they were, when they condemned himself; and how could he represent them? Whoever thought that this boy would be likely to speak of the subject of punishment in this school justly, might hold up his hand. Not a single hand was held up.

January 15th.—I arrived at five minutes past nine,

and found many of the children. All who were present were in their seats, attending to their lessons; and there were no words. At quarter of ten, Mr. Alcott began to read to the little children in Frank, and talked with them concerning the rights of private property.

He then, with her consent, told the rest how one of them had been tempted to take something which did not belong to her, and at first even took it; but by and by her conscience made her confess that she had it, and she gave it up. This was the story. This little girl went to a physician's house with a lame foot, and she found a very clean bandage on the floor, and she asked her father whose it was; and her father told her he supposed it was some lame person's bandage, or it belonged to the physician. The little girl kept unrolling and rolling up the bandage, and wanted to have it very much. At last she put it under her cloak, so that nobody might see, and soon slipped it into her pocket very cunningly. She thought her father did not see. So she sat there a little while to see how it would seem. She found it was very unpleasant. She thought the bandage did not belong to her; it belonged to somebody else. Her eyes looked strange. Her father did not say any thing. He thought her conscience would soon speak. She did not know that he had seen her put the bandage into her pocket. At last she felt she must say something. Father! said she, I am going to do something. Yes, said her father, I know it; and you had better do it now: so she took the bandage out, and said she did not want it, for it did not belong to her. And, when she went home, she told her mother she had come very near stealing! Mr. Alcott, after telling the story, asked the others if they ever took any thing; and they, and several more of the other class, acknowledged that they had sometimes. The lesson seemed to make a very serious impression.

At twenty minutes past ten the whole class turned for recitation. Mr. Alcott then began. Is it right for scholars to sit idle when they have time given them to study a particular lesson? No, sir, said several.

Mr. Alcott went to several children separately, and gave them certain directions about sitting right, not whispering, nor speaking loud, &c., and severally told them that if they were not obedient, they might lose the recess. He told them that this punishment was necessary, because they were weak, and needed this help to their inward strength. He then appointed a superintendent; for he said, though each one ought to be a superintendent of himself, the idea of a name's being written down on a slate had a wonderful influence, as we saw yesterday. The best children did not act differently, but the weak ones did; they needed this assistance, which answered a present good end.

A little boy turned round while the children were spelling, and did not attend to Mr. Alcott. Mr. Alcott called to him, and asked him where the words came from; if they did not come out of Mr. Alcott's mouth; and why he did not look at him. Then several words were defined and illustrated. *Trap* was illustrated figuratively in one instance; and Mr. Alcott said he hoped that the boy who was speaking had too much respect for his own mind ever to set traps for human minds. They all illustrated the word literally, by telling of the traps they set for each other in play. Mr. Alcott asked if they could tell why there was so much fun in setting traps. They did not explain it; and Mr. Alcott undertook to do so, by showing that it was the exercise of the understanding merely. But he asked why they thought of the pleasure of ingenuity, rather than sympathized with the boy caught, who was very often hurt or angry. They did not seem to know. The subject went farther, into the morality of sporting. The wickedness of cheating in school and in other cases was also discussed. At last it branched off into begging pardons, acknowledging faults, &c.; and the conversation extended to twelve o'clock, without the children's making any reference to the time of recess having come.

When speaking of traps, one boy said he heard of a trap Mr. Alcott had set. Mr. Alcott induced him to tell him. It was a story of something which happened in another school of Mr. Alcott's, and which one of the scholars had told to another boy, who had told it to a boy in this school. When it was finished, Mr. Alcott told the thing as it was; and it seemed that the principal point of the story, as it had been told, was false. Mr. Alcott said the boy referred to was a very bad one, and was at the school so short a time he had not become better. He then told several stories of boys in that town who were taken away from his school because they were punished, and sometimes just at the moment that the punishment had begun to alter their characters. He told one where a boy's punishment was to kneel to his companions, and acknowledge a fault. One or two said nothing would induce them to do that. I asked if, when they had injured others deeply, they would not delight to do any thing to repair it, and to show that they were sorry for it. And when they came to hear what the boy in question had done, and what traits of character he had displayed, they all agreed that the kneeling punishment was the only dignity in such a case.

After recess, Mr. Alcott put all but the first class in reading to their arithmetic lessons.

The piece selected for reading was from "Recollections of Childhood."

> I saw the infant cherub, — soft it lay,
> As it was wont, within its cradle, now
> Decked with sweet smiling flowers. A sight so strange
> Filled my young breast with wonder, and I gazed
> Upon the babe the more. I thought it slept, —
> And yet its little bosom did not move!
> I bent me down to look into its eyes,
> But they were closed; then softly clasped its hand,
> But mine it would not clasp. What should I do?
> "Wake, brother, wake!" I then impatient cried;
> "Open thine eyes, and look on me again!"
> He would not hear my voice. All pale beside
> My weeping mother sat, "and gazed and looked
> Unutterable things." "Will he not wake?"
> I eager asked. She answered but with tears
> Her eyes on me at length, with piteous look,

Were cast, — now on the babe once more were fixed,
And now on me; then, with convulsive sigh
And throbbing heart, she clasped me in her arms,
And in a tone of anguish faintly said,
"My dearest boy, thy brother does not sleep;
Alas! he's dead; he never will awake."
He's dead! I knew not what it meant, but more
To know I sought not. For the words so sad,
"He never will awake," sunk in my soul;
I felt a pang unknown before; and tears,
That angels might have shed, my heart dissolved.

Whose recollections are these? said Mr. Alcott. Mr. Pickering's, said one. What is the meaning of the word *recollect?* No answer. What is the meaning of *collect?* To bring together, said one. What, then, is the meaning of *recollect?* One said, to collect again. What did Mr. Pickering recollect? said Mr. Alcott. Some things he collected in childhood, said one. Are you now collecting or *re*-collecting the impressions of childhood? Some thought they had begun to *re*-collect, as well as to collect. Shall I tell you an idea some people have of recollecting, reminiscence, remembrance? Yes, said several of them. Mr. Alcott continued (pointing to the bust of Plato), That man believed that all our feelings and thoughts were the remembrances of another state of existence, before we came into the world in our present bodies. And he (pointing to the cast of Jesus Christ) used to say of himself that he came forth from God; that he had lived before. In the Gospel of St. John there are many passages in which he refers to his pre-existent state.

Mr. Alcott then began and read, "I thought it slept."

One of the boys said that he did not think it was right to say to the child that "he would never awake." Mr. Alcott said that the same thought had occurred to him as he was reading; that it was the moment when it would have been well to have told the child of the spiritual waking, and not to have let it stop with the idea of bodily death. The mother, however, only intended to say that the bodily eyes would never wake.

One boy said that he thought it impious to say, "And tears that angels might have shed my heart dissolved." Mr. Alcott asked, Why? He said, because the tears of a child are not good enough to be called angels' tears. Mr. Alcott said, It means they are innocent tears.

Another boy said that angels would not have wept, because they would have known about the life of the other world.

Mr. Alcott asked why the infant was called a cherub. They said, because it was good; because it was beautiful, &c. Mr. Alcott asked what idea they had of a cherub; and each answered according to his own ideas.

What is this piece of poetry about? said Mr. Alcott. Death, said one. Yes; the appearances to the senses when a spirit departs from the body of an infant. What were the appearances? The boy read the words, "the cradle," "the flowers," "the still body." What else is described? The feelings and sentiments these appearances produced, said one. Did these appearances produce the sentiments in the mind, or wake up sentiments which were already there? There was no answer to this question. Do the appearances carry the sentiments into the mind, or bring them out? One girl said, Carry them in; a boy at the same moment said, Bring them out. Mr. Alcott asked if there were any sentiments in the outward world. The girl immediately changed her mind.

Why did Mr. Pickering "gaze the more"? One said, because he "thought it slept." What did he observe as he gazed the more? That "its bosom did not move." What did he then do? He tried to look into the eyes. How were they? "Closed." What did he do next? He "took his hand." What did he seem to expect? That it would "clasp his;" but it did not. What was his feeling then? He did not know what to do, and he addressed the body impatiently. And what then took place? The baby "would not hear his voice." Why did Mr. Pickering think he would not; where did he get that thought? He thought the spirit was still there. Yes, said Mr. Alcott. It is the spirit that wills; and to whom did his mind then turn? To his mother. How did she look? "Pale and weeping." And it seemed to typify what it was not possible to voice out, said Mr. Alcott; but do you think there are any unutterable things in your spirit? A little girl said after a long pause, Yes. Mr. Alcott said, Yes, there are some unutterable things in every mind — feelings, not thoughts; so feeling is finer and deeper than thought. Were all the deepest feelings bodied forth in sculpture, or painting, or in things, or voiced out in words, what would it all be? After a pause two spoke at once, and said, God. They meant that complete expression of all inward life would be a full manifestation of God. Thus they made feelings as well as thoughts synonymous with spirit.

What else does Mr. Pickering say of the mother? "Tears." What are tears? Expressions of unutterable things. All tears? No, some are on trifling occasions. Are you ashamed of your tears? Sometimes. "Jesus wept," said Mr. Alcott, and it was on a similar occasion, when there was death. What else did the mother do? She "clasped him." Why? Because she was glad that he was alive. What else did she do? "She sighed." Yes, another emblem of an agitated spirit.

In this way, Mr. Alcott went on over every particular of the description, and the lesson continued for an hour and a half, of which I have given above not the most interesting, or the largest part, as I forgot I was writing, many times.

January 16*th.* — When I arrived at quarter past nine, I found the children quietly seated at their lessons. One of the girls handed me a note, in answer to one I had written to her expressing my pleasure in her moral progress after we had had occasion to blame her a good deal. It expressed gratitude to Mr. Alcott and me for not sparing her faults. Such demonstrations are the instructor's true reward.

At half-past nine Mr. Alcott took his little class. They looked very animated. Mr. Alcott said, You seem to look very much pleased when I come to read to you. They all smiled. He began, "A few days after." What is a few? Two or three. "His mother called Frank!" You know Frank always looked when his mother said Frank; do you always look when your father and mother speak your name? Sometimes, said they. She said, Get your hat. What do you think Frank did? He got his hat instantly, and he went along jumping and singing. What did he jump and sing for? Because he was glad, &c., &c.

It is impossible to follow these reading lessons. To hear Mr. Alcott read at least once, would give a better idea of it than pages of description. Every sentence is addressed to the children, and required back from them; and there is no point of morality or conduct touched on which is not taken up and applied, and wandering eyes are steadied as an exercise in self-control. After this lesson is read, the little children turn round to their desks, and are encouraged to make letters and pictures on their tablets, from the models which are scattered over their desks in profusion. Books of pictures are also there, and they are led in this way to exercise their eyes upon forms, to their great advantage, it being the most excellent preparation for all their future studies. Mr. Alcott requires them to be so still as not to interrupt or disturb the school; but that is all. They are constantly amused and engaged, and seem perfectly happy. They often turn round to hear what Mr. Alcott tells or reads to the other children, especially if he reads stories.

Mr. Alcott then took the smaller division of the class, and spelled and defined the words, and talked to them on the subjects brought up by the lesson. *Wise*, said he, means to have good feelings and good thoughts, and to act them out. If you have no good feelings or good thoughts, you are not wise; and even if you have good feelings and good thoughts, and you do not act them out, you are not wise. *Wisp* was one of the words; and, to illustrate it, he read that passage of the "Story without an End," where the child sees the Will-o'-the-Wisp.

At ten minutes past ten, the spelling lesson began, after he had placed the chairs of the smaller division very far apart from each other, so that the children should not be tempted to whisper. One boy was made the superintendent; and Mr. Alcott said to him, You know you cannot put down a name because you wish to, nor refrain from putting it down because you do not wish to. Conscience must write down the names, not inclination. There is the responsibility of each boy's pleasure for half an hour resting on you; do you understand? Yes.

Now all define or illustrate silence by action, or rather by no action. There was a pause. We are going to name thoughts, feelings, and actions, or to word them. Is *tree* the wording of a thought, person, action, feeling, or thing? A thing. Is *trim* the wording of a thing, person, action, or feeling? An action. All the words were thus half defined. Then they were spelled; and, what is very uncommon, three words were spelled wrong. The words were afterwards defined and illustrated.

When the word *vast* was defined, Mr. Alcott asked if the idea of vastness was within or without? Several answered, both. Some said, within. One hesitated, and Mr. Alcott asked, what was vast? He said, the ocean. Mr. Alcott asked if the ocean did not wake up the idea of vast in his mind. He replied, Yes, and so vastness is in the mind. What, then, is the ocean? said Mr. Alcott. An emblem of vastness, said the boy. The ocean, then, is the external, visible, material sign, type, or emblem, of the internal, invisible, spiritual idea of vastness; is it? This definition was repeated, in nearly the same words, by two of the class.

The word *veil* led to a consideration of the body as the veil of the spirit, and of the earth as the veil of many of the ideas of God. When was the veil of sense wrapped round our souls? said Mr. Alcott. When we were born, said one. When will it be taken away? When we die, said several. Cannot the veil be raised till we die? After a while, it was seen, and said, that the veil could be raised by being born again out of sense into thoughts or spirit, — by insight. Mr. Alcott then repeated the passage from St. Paul about being caught up to the third heaven, and asked them whether the veil was raised for that man. They said, Yes. He then said that the object of this school was to unveil the soul; and he was glad to hear that one of the scholars had said, out of school, that it was impossible to remain in it, and not learn to know one's self.

January 16*th.* — When the children were arranged to spell, Mr. Alcott began: Such of you as feel an interest in this lesson, hold up your hands. All did. Why? One boy said, Because it teaches us to spell, and gives us meanings of words. Another said, Because of the conversations that arise. Why are these conversations interesting? said Mr. Alcott. Because they give us new ideas, replied the boy. Many others said they liked them for the same reason. Mr. Alcott then said, Conversations are the most perfect transcript of mind. Could the conversations of great men be recorded, it would give us a better idea of them than any history of their lives. Why is the New Testament so interesting? Because it is full of the conversations of Jesus. And the conversations of Socrates make perhaps the next most interesting book in the world. Conversation is full of life; for the spirit's workings come out in conversation, fresh and vivid.

He now appointed a superintendent; and, seeing a boy laughing without apparent reason, he said he might write down any smiles that did not arise out of the subject of the lesson; for smiles indicate a state of mind, and, when something is in the mind which has no relation to the subject, it is out of place. Besides, several take up the smile, and attention is diverted. It is true that smiles may arise out of the subject, and then they are proper. One boy said, If we had longer words, we should have more interesting conversations. Mr. Alcott said, The short words have the most meaning in them; and he illustrated this by a great many instances.

He then took the spelling lesson and began to talk, and make observations upon the scholars, illustrating the first word *work* in every variety of application, literal and figurative; and he went on in this talk, bringing in every word of the lesson, in various meanings. The children soon caught the idea, and joined in, and made sentences also, as they arose in their minds, in which the words were applied figuratively, according to their fancies. Lines of poetry were also quoted. It would not be possible to follow this desultory conversation, although it was conducted with perfect order. At one point of it (the word *yean*) Mr. Alcott took down Wordsworth, and read "Barbara Leithwaite," in which this word occurred. When he had read this half through, he laid down the book; but they begged him to finish it, and he took it up again, and read the story through.

Yelk, he said, was the food by which the germ of life was nourished into the power of forming a body that might individualize it; and he said the earth (perhaps) was the yelk by which souls were nourished or born into a consciousness of the spiritual life. He explained this a little. All eyes were fixed upon him almost constantly. Neither a sense of duty alone, nor the attraction of the speaker alone, could explain the profound attention of these children. But the combination of the two causes is irresistible. And Mr. Alcott requires them to seem attentive, as well as to be attentive. He often talks to them on the possibility and the duty of making every part of their body express the thought of their minds, and tells them that they must not accuse people of injustice who interpret their automatic movements and careless habits.

The word *yawn* led to some amusing anecdotes about yawning; but he soon arrested them, and said, that was enough. He added, however, that he liked amusing stories; and he thought these should be intermingled with serious stories, in right proportion — but stories of one kind made the mind one-sided.

After Mr. Alcott had illustrated all the words of the lesson by this conversation, he took the dictionary and read Johnson's definitions, to see how much resemblance there was; and this led to further remarks on the words. He then heard the words spelled, and asked each one to give a short definition.

Every day he varies the mode of this lesson, in order that it may not sink into a routine. There was a hesitation at the word *yean.* Mr. Alcott said, The earth yeans its millions of productions. To give birth to, was immediately responded. Mr. Alcott said yeanling meant a young one until it was weaned.

Zeal was defined by one of the boys, to feel so much as to set the will a-going. A recent scholar, a little boy, whispered once, in the course of the hour and a half; and Mr. Alcott said, Little boy, do you know that you break the rules of this school when you whisper? He then remarked that to want to do any thing, was no reason at all for doing it; the question was, does God want it to be done? — While I was attending to the Latin, after recess, Mr. Alcott gave lessons in Arithmetic and English Grammar.

January 17*th.*—I arrived before nine, and found some of the scholars at their seats, and also heard some Geometry lessons. I then looked over, in order to read, my journal of the last week, while the class were spelling their lesson, omitting the defining of the words. As soon as the spelling was done, I read the journal of the week past; and they were very attentive indeed. The idea of having this Journal read, seems to create a happy influence on the school. No one defends his faults when he sees himself in the Journal. It is evidently a great aid to self-knowledge.

Mr. Alcott then prepared to read in the Bible. He appointed a superintendent, and made some remarks on the assistance a superintendent gave to the weak. I am going to read about One, said he, of whose thoughts, actions, and feelings you always delight to hear; whom you are reminded of by that cast (pointing to it); for that is a representation of the body out of which he looked. All spirits, in this world, are in bodies; his was; just as your spirits are in your bodies. Well, this one said, "I and my Father are one;" he did not mean one body, but one spirit; that they had the same thoughts and feelings; all pure spirits, all real spirits, must have the same thoughts and feelings, must be one with God; all that is truly spiritual in your souls is one with God. But the Jews did not understand him when he said that he and his Father were one. The people around him thought less of their spirits, than about bodies;

so they did not understand him (perhaps they did not try, said he, very expressively, addressing one boy of an inactive mind). And they replied, You do not speak truly, in saying that you are God! Now he did not mean his body, but they did not attend to see what he meant; they misunderstood, as some thoughtless boys do here when I speak in pictures. And they took up stones to stone him. But he said, Remember what works you have seen me do; I have done a great many good works among you, such as God would do; and I did them to show you what works God does; I have done many compassionate, kind works; for which one of these works are you going to stone me? They said, We do not stone you for your good works, but for saying you are God. Jesus said, But in your own books, that you believe in, it is said, "Ye are gods." I say nothing new when I say that my spirit is one with God's. All spirits are of God, as you already know; and why do you say I do not speak true, when I say I am the Son of God; especially since my works are such as He would do? If I do not such works as God does, I do not want you to believe me spiritual; but the works! believe, attend to, think about them; and they will convince you that I am in the Father, and the Father in me. Then they sought to take him, but he walked away. And why did they seek to take him? They did not understand that the spirit in them was of God; they did not want to feel obliged to look into themselves; they preferred to attend to their bodies. Perhaps they did not understand him; but it was only because they did not try; it is our duty to try. Jesus went away to the place where John used to put water on the bodies of such as intended to be good, as an emblem of the cleansing of mind which he taught.

Jesus soon had an opportunity to prove what he said about the spirit's being one with God. A friend of his died; it was the brother of Mary and Martha. That was the Mary who had anointed the Lord with ointment, and wiped his feet with her hair. A messenger came to Jesus and said, "He whom you love is sick." Jesus said to those about him, I do not grieve for it; for by this sickness of Lazarus, I shall be able to show you that the spirit is one with God, that it cannot die; and I am glad that God may be brought out to your eyes, by a display of spiritual power. And he stayed two days where he was, and then he said, Let us go into Judea again.

Now his friends remembered the stoning, and they said What! will you go where you will be killed; where your body will be hurt, will be stoned? Yes, he said, I shall go. Our friend Lazarus sleeps; I go that I may wake him out of his sleep. His disciples said, "If he sleep, he shall do well:" they meant, if he only sleeps, for they did not understand that Jesus meant the sleep of death. Then Jesus said (for he saw they did not understand him), He is dead. And I am glad of it for your sake: for now I shall be able to make you understand the spirit's life, — that part of us which is one with God, and that cannot die. Mr. Alcott paraphrased the whole story thus; but I could not keep up with my pen. The children were profoundly attentive, and deeply impressed.

January 20*th.* — I was not well and did not come; and for this I was very sorry, for Mr. Alcott reviewed all the spelling lessons of the last six weeks, and it was very interesting, he said, to see how the words brought up, by association, the past illustrations and conversations. Mr. Alcott said he was delighted to find how the little ones had been benefited by the ideas, and how they recalled the most important, as soon as they looked at the words. He had had every reason to believe that these conversations were useful, from their expression of attention at the moment; but it was an additional gratification to find that the most general and ideal conversations were remembered most distinctly. For it was most worthy of remark, in the review, that the most general views and the most ideal pictures were those which had seized most strongly on the minds of the younger children.

January 21*st.* — I arrived at a little after nine.

Mr. Alcott showed me Peale's Graphics, which, he said, had brought out beautifully the theory of chirography which he had long attempted to put in practice; and had connected it with drawing. I looked over it and found that it was the very thing for this school.

Mr. Alcott first read to the little class of four, and then took the younger division of the spelling class. One of the boys said, Mr. Alcott, I have learned my lesson; on which Mr. Alcott, taking up a book, imitated the manner in which a child tried to study with the lips without the mind. They all laughed: and he then explained study to be thinking about words, until pictures were formed in their minds; and he ridiculed the humming, buzzing, whispering over the words, moving the body, &c., by imitating it himself; and when he asked if they understood him, if they agreed with his views, if they had had such habits, if they had any of these still, if they saw their folly, if they would give them all up, &c., they all confessed, and seemed disposed to reform. He then described how this lesson should be studied, how they could think beforehand of illustrating the words in sentences, and convinced them that to learn the spelling lesson thoroughly would require the whole hour assigned to it. He said that a great variety of exercises on words were coming. Next week he should vary the mode of considering words; for it was necessary to apply the mind in new ways to this subject, in order that they should not forget to think.

Mr. Alcott then said, that if any were inattentive during the lesson, if they did not behave well, he should deprive them of instruction after recess. He then spoke of the importance of looking at him, in order to catch the full meanings that went from him.

A girl then said, Mr. Alcott, I wonder how it is that we sit here over the spelling lesson as long as we are in church, and yet I am never the least fatigued; while, in church, I am so tired, and we have to sit as still here as there. The rest agreed with her in wondering how it was. Mr. Alcott said it was because their own minds were active here, and activity of mind made the blood circulate, and the whole body feel vigorous. He said it was one of his great objects to call forth the soul in action, to govern the body. He spoke of manners, and said that, for good manners, there must be both refined minds and the early acquired habit of letting the mind govern the body.

The words were spelled first; they were of five letters. Every word was spelled right. The little boys were then told to take their spelling-books, and hold their fingers on each word while these were illustrated.

The most interesting word was *black*, in its figurative meanings, as wicked, sad. It was spoken of as the color for mourning, and Mr. Alcott said he thought it was unfortunate that this color should be used when people's friends left this world. He spoke of the custom of burning the dead and keeping the dust, and of other methods of removing the sad ideas of decay which it is best to separate from death. We observed that the children had no sad ideas of death, and that they generally thought it was rather a subject of joy than of grief.

There was a talk with one boy who made objection to the encroachment upon the recess; and Mr. Alcott said that this boy thought it was wrong to lose one moment's play, but he did not think it wrong to occupy ever so much time in school hours with unnecessary opposition. He said were it not for his health, he should deprive him entirely of recess on account of his encroachments upon school hours.

After recess, the youngest scholars were employed, some in drawing, and some in arithmetic. The rest were formed into a large semicircle, for an analysis of the passage, " Stay thy soft murmuring waters, gentle rill ;" quoted by Miss Edgeworth from Darwin.

The scale was made, and Mr. Alcott asked them if they thought the word *objects* was the best name for such words as were generally put in that column. Some thought that the word *things* would be better; but, on further reflection, perceived it would not be so general as the word *objects*. He then asked what they thought about that word *actions*. *Movements*, *stirrings*, *changes*, were suggested ; *acts* was decided upon.

After the analysis was finished, he asked them whether the objects in this passage were external or internal. External. What sort of poetry is this? External, worldly, material, were the various answers. He at last led them to say, descriptive.

When pointing out questions, they always told what object or action was qualified. When they noted a substitute, they told what word it was substituted for; and the relations were explained.

After it was over, Mr. Alcott explained to them that this was grammar, and every thing in language could be learned without the words *verbs*, *nouns*, *tenses*, &c. One of the children asked why then they should ever learn those words. Mr. Alcott told them, for the convenience of learning other languages. They then retired to their seats, and some remarks were made on order. Mr. Alcott said, There are two persons here who are always very orderly. Several children immediately named two of the scholars.

January 22d. — I arrived late. When the little class was arranged, Mr. Alcott said he should read a short lesson. One said he wanted a long one. Mr. Alcott said that might be, if their minds did not wander away.

Then the younger division of the spelling lesson spelled, and he told them to take their books, and keep their fingers on the words as the rest of the class spelled and talked about them. The class turned and arranged themselves very quietly.

What ideas does the word *blade* bring into your mind? said Mr. Alcott. A spire of grass, and the part of the knife that cuts, said one. The next added, a gay young man; the next, a sword; the next, a scythe. Another boy said, A blade may be a figurative expression for the mind when it is sharpened by wisdom. Another said, the shoulder-blade. The next said, a pair of scissors. Mr. Alcott then read Johnson's definition, and spoke of the blades of corn, and quoted the expression, "first the blade, then the ear then the full corn in the ear."

What ideas do you connect with the word *blame?* To reproach, said one. What is reproach? Find fault with, said the next. Blame is speaking ill of, said the next; and the next said, to accuse one of being the means of something wrong being done. One little boy said, to blame was to punish; another said it was to scold. Mr. Alcott then read Johnson's definition, and the definitions of all the derivatives. He then asked those who thought they were blameless to hold up their hands. No one held up his hand, but one boy said his minister was blameless. Mr. Alcott said he was glad he had so high an idea of him. The next boy pointed to the cast of Christ as the only blameless one. Mr. Alcott said to a boy who did not like to be blamed, that it was a great character which could receive blame without resentment. Another boy said that he could never be blamed without being angry. Mr. Alcott said, that was just his fault. A good deal was said of bearing blame meekly, even when deserved.

After a while Mr. Alcott asked two of the scholars if they did not think that, a few months before, they were too apt to be angry when they were blamed, and to defend themselves when they were really in the wrong? They both confessed. Mr. Alcott said they had entered the Wicket gate, and the burden had loosened from their backs; for that he never saw any children who were such extraordinary instances of the determination not to be found fault with; and that, if they had got over that, they had accomplished more than if they had learned a whole science. He was glad that they had made progress.

Bliss was defined as the highest degree of pleasure. One boy remarked that pleasure had once before been defined as the enjoyment of the body, and happiness as the enjoyment of the mind. Another boy said bliss was the pleasure of the body and mind; indeed, he thought pleasure and happiness were the same: Mr. Alcott said he did not like to have these things confounded, and that he thought it was only when all the pleasures of the body were lost in the happiness of the mind that there was bliss. He spoke of the pleasures of the body as interfering with those of the mind, by overtasking the body. He asked those who thought they knew what bliss was, to hold up their hands. Some did. He then asked why we were so made as to delight in pleasure. As no one replied, he answered, that by the disappointment which it involved, it led us to seek for real happiness. He spoke of Hercules's choice. He then asked those who thought they had ever mistaken pleasure for happiness, to hold up their hands. Some did. Mr. Alcott said, Pleasure is the divinity of earth, and bliss descends from heaven. He allowed, however, that pleasure may typify bliss.

Bloat, he said, was a good word to follow this conversation; for pleasure sometimes bloats. It was defined as swelling out; an intoxicated man was bloated. By pleasure, said Mr. Alcott, or by happiness? By pleasure, said several at once.

Brace was defined, and carried into its figurative meanings, of strengthening the mind, &c.; and virtue was said to brace body and mind. These were the most interesting words.

January 24th.—I arrived a few minutes after nine, and found them in their seats at a writing lesson. Mr. Alcott went round and round, looking at their writing, till quarter of ten. When he had read to the little class as usual, he asked those of the other class who had not whispered to turn round. Only ten turned, and none of the older scholars had been silent. Mr. Alcott then asked some of the scholars, calling them by name, for what they came up to the Temple to-day. One boy did not answer. Another said, To come to school. Mr. Alcott asked why he came to school. As there was no answer, he said that the object for which boys generally went to school was to study the sciences; but he hoped that all who came here knew that they came not only for science, but to study themselves. He then asked a very good boy what he thought he came to school for. He said, To improve his mind and heart. (A little boy here began to move about, and Mr. Alcott told him he had troubled him for several days, and now he should take him out of the room for correction, in order to save the necessity of harder punishment by and by; which he did.)

When he came back, a little girl was asked what she came for; if she came merely for the lessons. She said, No. Mr. Alcott said, You come here to learn how to behave at home; I do not mean to learn how to make bows and courtesies, but to feel and think better. And then he said if any had begun to be conscious that they treated their parents at home with more feeling, from having more feeling, than they used to do, they might hold up their hands. Many held up their hands. Some thought they could not care more for their parents than they did now. To one boy who thought so, Mr. Alcott said that when he never disobeyed them, when he cared as much for their wishes as his own, he might say he could not love them any better, but not till then.

I read my Journal, and they all agreed that no injustice had been done to them in the Journal, though one boy said that two things seemed to him to have been stated differently from the fact; he could not remember what they were, however.

Mr. Alcott then proposed to read, and gave five minutes grace, during which several children went out. After having read a story of jealousy and malignity on the one side, and of generosity and long-suffering on the other, he asked those who thought they knew what this spirit of generosity and long-suffering was, to hold up their hands. Several did. Who among you has exercised it? said he. One boy alone held up his hand, at which the rest smiled. Mr. Alcott thought that all present might find scope for the exercise of this feeling every day, at home and in school. Mr. Alcott then asked, What is forbearance? One boy answered, bearing things for others; another said, bearing other people's malice patiently, and doing good to them. Does bearing and forbearing come from the body or the mind? From the mind. Which is uppermost when you bear or forbear? The heart. Did you ever give up one of your body's wants, because it was right? said he to a little boy, who was doing something wrong. Yes. He added that the measure of goodness might be taken, in any person, by seeing how much they sacrificed their body's wants to those of the mind. No person was good who found that he could not sacrifice his body's wants to those of the mind. Every boy might judge himself, by reflecting how much and how easily he sacrificed his body's wants to those of the mind. He wished they would all think in their own minds how much goodness they had, according to this test.

After recess the children came in and took their seats, from the anteroom and from the Common. A boy brought up his journal, which he had just begun; and Mr. Alcott remarked that he was one who had begun to learn to write by printing, and therefore, though his hand was not yet strong enough to make his writing graceful, yet the distinctness of the writing showed that the idea of every letter was right in his mind. He added that he always found this distinctness in the writing of those who began with printing.

He then read this journal to himself at the boy's request, and afterwards the other journals aloud. He told one journalist that he wished he would put more of himself into the journal; the boy of that journal, was a mere automaton; he came in, and went out, and did things, but he never felt or thought. He took up another boy's journal next, because the boy seemed to be very anxious to have his journal read; Mr. Alcott found great difficulty in reading his handwriting, and at last had to give it up; and he advised the boy to print for a month, all the time, in order to give some clearness to his handwriting. Mr. Alcott then said that four of them might either give up writing the journal, and write printed letters (the best way to learn to write), or write the script hand better and more clearly.

A great deal of movement, unnecessary speaking, &c., interrupted Mr. Alcott in all his conversations this morning. So he stopped reading the journals, and went around and told what boys and girls he had faith in, and what boys and girls he had not faith in. There seemed to be a general sense of justice in his classification. He said that he had been so much interrupted to-day that he should retain some of the scholars after school. This produced a perfect silence, during which time he told a story to illustrate the grounds of having faith in others.

Mr. Alcott praised the writing of one of the girls in her journal, and said that the journal gave something of her mind. One of the four boys whose writing had been blamed did not seem to like it that she should be praised; and to fear that Mr. Alcott omitted to mention all her bad spelling. Mr. Alcott said two words were spelled wrong, but there were a great many words wrong in his journal, which he had omitted to mention, because he thought it would make him angry; for he had said, a day or two before, he could not have his faults pointed out, without being angry. Another girl's journal was full of her thoughts and feelings, very much superior to any journal we have had; and Mr. Alcott praised it, but she was not present to-day.

January 26th. — At ten o'clock, Mr. Alcott called on the class of spelling to rise, and fix their blackboards, and write the spelling lesson to his dictation with their chalk pencils. This afforded occasion for remarks on their writing. It takes two things, said he, to make a good writer; one is a clear conception of beautiful forms in the mind, and another is the skill to guide the hand. Some persons have one of these qualities without the other. He recommended a careful study of the forms in Peale's Graphics, and a great deal of practice; telling them how, when he was a child, he was fond of printing on the snow, in the sand, &c.

When they came to the word *brain*, in the spelling lesson, Mr. Alcott asked, what was the difference between the brain and the mind? One boy said, The brain, when not used figuratively, means a part of the head, and the mind means the seat of learning and thought. Another said, The brain is the soft part of the head, the inside; and the mind is the hard part of the head. Mr. Alcott asked him if he thought that matter could think. He said, No. Mr. Alcott said, But you think the mind is matter, if you think it is the hard part of the head. A small boy here said, Is not the brain the case of the mind? and another boy answered him, The brain is the seed of the mind. Two little boys said the brain was the sense; one girl said it was the understanding. Mr. Alcott said, I should say the brain is the instrument by which the spirit acts; from which remark ensued a long conversation, to meet the difficulties of the older children, who had confounded the mind with its organs; and the subject, not being exhausted at half-past eleven, was left to be resumed another day, as the recess hour was come, and the time after recess was devoted to Latin and arithmetic.

January 27th. — The subject of the brain was resumed, and the materialist of yesterday was brought to discriminate the mind from its organs, by the question, whether he thought that when the soul ascended, the brain went with it. The truth was, that it was only a disputatious spirit which had made him fight off the right idea so long. Mr. Alcott closed by asking those who thought the mind and the brain were not the same thing to hold up their hands; and all held up their hands.

January 28th. — When the school turned, at ten o'clock, to face Mr. Alcott, he said, All who have whispered this morning may turn back. All the girls and some of the boys turned back. All who have asked unnecessary questions may turn back. Several more turned. He then said, Now those who have not whispered, but consulted their own memories about their places, and depended on me to supply them with all they wanted, without asking questions, may rise. They did so, and he said, These are my scholars; the rest keep schools of their own. After some little talk, all agreed to give up their schools, and go to Mr. Alcott's. He explained the bearing of all his rules on their habits of mind and character; and they all acknowledged their propriety.

He then said that he was going to read some pictures of what goes on in the mind during the period of its development on earth, by means of the duties of life;

but if one boy or girl interrupts me, said he, I shall stop; and that boy or girl will bring a deprivation upon the whole school; those who are innocent being obliged to suffer, as the good are always willing to do, for the instruction of the guilty. This remark elicited some doubts, which were settled by reference to Christ, and all martyrs and self-sacrificing philanthropists, who have made it their vocation on earth to seek and save, even if they suffer and die for the truth.

At last, the "Faery Queene" was opened, and Mr. Alcott began: Goodness may be said to be at war with Wickedness; and Spenser has pictured out Goodness as a knight who goes forth into the world to combat with enemies. When I read about St. George, you may understand that he represents Goodness; his enemies are the enemies of Goodness. I shall first read about St. George's combating with Error, one of the first enemies that Goodness meets with in the world.

He then read or rather paraphrased the description of Una, and told them that she represented Truth. She "inly mourned" because Wickedness and Error existed; she was "in white," because Truth is pure, bright, and innocent. He read the account of the Wood of Error and the adventure in it, in a very free paraphrase, interweaving the explanation of the allegory. They listened with the most intense interest, and could not help exclaiming, as they sympathized in the various turns of the battle. At the end of the battle he stopped, and asked them if he should go on; and they all exclaimed, Go on, go on. He went on, and read of the meeting with Hypocrisy, up to the scene in the House of Sleep. When he had finished, he asked, What has this taught you? One boy said, To resist evil. Mr. Alcott then went on to speak of the conflict of good and evil within themselves, and made individual applications which brought the subject home to each one's own experience.

January 29th. — At the usual hour for spelling, he called on those that had not broken one rule about whispering to turn round. All turned but five. He commended the conscientiousness of these five in not turning round, but said that they were wrong in breaking the rules. He then said to the rest that if any of them had turned without examining themselves, they had deceived, had injured their souls, and commenced the career of falsehood. He enlarged upon falsehood and its consequences, and at last two girls turned back. The rest remained firm; and Mr. Alcott said he considered these as his scholars, for they obeyed his rules. The others kept their own schools, and had their own rules, at least for to-day, and might keep their faces turned from him. He told the class to take their spelling-books; and he called on several scholars to pronounce the words they had been studying, and they did so. He then spoke of pronunciation; its importance.

A long conversation ensued on the word *blush*, which each of the children illustrated by sentences; and it was remarked, that the comparison which the soul makes of its own ideal with the actual, naturally produces an excitement in the mind, which the body expresses by a blush.

The word *brass* being illustrated by the sentence, "An impudent person is said to have brass," led to a still further illustration of the signs of mental delicacy.

The word *brave* led to a long disquisition upon true and false courage; during which a passage was read from "My Early Days."

January 30*th.*—After the writing lesson was over, and the children were all turned to listen, Mr. Alcott spoke of the duty of forming the habit of attention; its usefulness in fitting them to be benefited by lectures, of which there were so many, and which were of so little use to most who heard them, on account of their want of power to attend. Then he desired them to think, as he asked a few questions, preparatory to the subject of the reading.

What do you mean by *birthday?* said he.

The day on which you are born, said one. What do you mean by being born? Coming into the world. What comes into the world? A person. What is a person? The body and mind of a child. Which comes into the world, body or mind? Body.

Birthday is the day on which the spirit is put into the body, said another boy. Did you get that idea in this school? said Mr. Alcott. I never thought of such subjects before I came to this school, said he.

Birthday is the day when the soul and body meet together the first time, said another boy. It is the day when the soul takes the body and comes into the world, said a very small boy. Do you mean that the soul brings the body, or the body brings the soul? The soul brings the body.

Another little boy said, The soul comes from heaven; the day it comes is its birthday.

A little girl here said she thought soul and body began on the same day. One of the boys added, that he had always had an indistinct idea that the soul lived before the body, that there was a transmigration of souls. A little boy said, God makes the body and soul separate, but at the same time, and puts them together afterwards. Mr. Alcott heard them all, and then said, Those who believe the soul lives before the body, hold up your hands. All did, except a few; but some did not. Mr. Alcott asked those who did not, if they thought soul and body were made at the same minute. One said, Yes. The rest said they thought soul was made first.

Now go forth into the external world, said Mr. Alcott, and find some fact or appearance in the external world with which to picture out and typify birth. They were quite animated by this, and the following were the most striking analogies. One said, The seed sown, and springing up. What do you mean by the seed, body or soul? Both. Another said, The branches from the trunk. The soul is the trunk, and the branches the body. Another said, I should think the trunk was God, and the branches were the soul. Another said, The soul is a rose-bud putting forth leaves. Another said, God is a rock, and we are pieces broken off.

Violently? No, not violently. The next said, God is the water, and our souls are drops; he afterwards added, that God was the only real person, and we were pictures of him. God is the ocean, and we are the rivers, said the next. Another said, God is a sower, and we are the seeds which he sows. Another boy said, The seed is God, and we are the fruit that springs out of it. Another said, God is the earth, and we are the productions. Another said, God is the Shepherd, and we are the sheep. Mr. Alcott said, That is Scripture phraseology; but Jesus is generally called the Shepherd. One of the little girls said, God is the Sun, and Jesus Christ is the Moon, and we are stars. You mean, said Mr. Alcott, that Jesus is superior to us, and God is superior to all, and gives his light to Jesus? Yes. That is the best one of all, said the rest. I then remarked that I had lately heard our soul compared to a river of thoughts and feelings, pouring through us from God, the Eternal Fountain, and augmented in the course of our mortal life, by other rivers from the same source.

Mr. Alcott allowed these analogies to run on, that they all might clearly understand the principle of metaphor. At last he said, These are analogies, and many of them are good, but none are perfect; for there is nothing in the vegetable or animal world which is quite adequate to typify the great fact of birth, the incarnation, or embodying of spirit. The internal eye sees this fact; the external eye cannot see it. You have expressed by your analogies that the soul comes from

God: do you think that when it first appears, in the human form, it is pure, innocent? All held up their hands. Do you think that those who have lived in the world awhile, that you, any of you, are as good as you were when you were infants? None thought so. So you think that you grow worse as you live on? They generally thought that they saw vice, and tried it, to see how it would seem. One girl said, When we are babies we do not know. Mr. Alcott said, Is knowledge the cause of evil? Do you remember the beautiful illustration of the beginning of sin in the Old Testament, the tree of knowledge and the tree of life; or the fruits of the head, and the fruits of the heart? One boy said, We are brought up to think the old do right, and when we see them do wrong, we think it is right, and imitate them. Is it irresistible to imitate the old? said Mr. Alcott. They all said, No. He then read from the "Boston Observer" the lines called a "Birthday Blessing," and said, These lines were written to a little boy, by the lady who keeps the Journal of our school.

Thou spirit bright! though wishes only show
How weak we are, how little 'tis we know,
My heart will wish that childhood's sacred power
Could still prolong *for thee* its consecrating hour.

Yet what is time? I know the spirit pure
That breathes in childhood's bosom may endure
The shock of years; and that its sunny eye
Doth tell of that within which may refuse to die.

For childhood's bosom is the poet's dream;
The soul undarkened yet by earth; the gleam

Of light that was in paradise; the tree
Whose fruit is genius, power, and immortality!

But ah! how many turn aside and eat
The tree of death! Unfortified to meet
The giant-spirit of the earth, they die
To all that makes life blest, beneath his withering eye!

Oh! rush not thou so blindly into life,
Nor ask too early for the giant strife;
Still dwell secure, while love and joy grow strong,
'Mid childhood's trusting prayers, and sacred fear of wrong.

'Tis thus the saint, the hero, and the sage,
Preserve the unfallen man from age to age,
With childhood's asking heart still looking up,
Till He, the Source of Good, hath filled the o'erflowing cup.

And hence the artist and the poet draw
Their power to charm, to elevate, to awe;
Faithful to childhood's love and instincts, lo!
On beauty calling, paradise again doth glow!

And is it thus? And is the gifted eye
The unfettered flow of pure humanity?
And doth the Eternal Beauty, Truth and Good,
Thus o'er the fountain-head of soul forever brood?

Then ever be a child! in this one prayer
I ask for all the loftiest man can share;
The spirit free from custom's "frosty weight,"
And open to each thought that makes our being great.

When he read the lines, —

And doth the Eternal Beauty, Truth and Good,
Thus o'er the fountain-head of soul forever brood? —

he stopped, and asked if they knew what that meant. They said, Yes, it means God, because the soul comes from him. Mr. Alcott then repeated Jesus Christ's remarks about his own origin, and about childhood; and closed with reading the lines from Wordsworth beginning, —

Our birth is but a sleep, and a forgetting.

January 31*st.* — Mr. Alcott chose for his readings from the Bible such passages as would bring up again and again the idea that Jesus considered childhood innocent, and that innocence is a positive condition; that it comprehends all the instincts and feelings which naturally tend to good, such as humility, self-forgetfulness, love, trust, &c.; and that the true method of self-cultivation is to retain these feelings or return to the childish state and reproduce them. He began: "And they brought to Jesus little children," and went on to the expression, "Of such is the kingdom of heaven," and through the story of the young man who lacked, and the parable of the laborers who all had a penny. He made some applications of this parable to those present. Then he read the parables illustrating forgiveness, and asked how many had this spirit of forgiveness. Some held up their hands. Mr. Alcott went on to speak of forgiveness, and said, when they yielded in a quarrel, and forbore, they were not yielding to this or that boy, but to God; and when they fought with a fellow-being they were fighting against God. As this seemed to strike the children with astonishment, Mr.

Alcott referred to Jesus Christ's expression, "Inasmuch as ye do it unto the least of these little ones, ye do it unto me." He then read the account of Christ's entrance into Jerusalem, and the expression, "Out of the mouths of babes and sucklings God hath perfected praise," which he explained to mean the innocent expressions of pure childhood, in word and deed.

Now, said he, I am going to read what will show how a child may be perverted; and he read the story of the Pharisee and Publican (in paraphrase as usual), up to the place where Jesus said that, "whosoever will not receive the kingdom of heaven as a little child, shall not enter it." He then read the conversation with Nicodemus.

After recess, I called a little boy to me, and asked him if he thought he had improved since he came here. He said, Yes. How? do you think any more? Why, I did not know I could think, before I came here! What did you do before, all the time? I am sure I don't know. Mr. Alcott talked a little with one of the girls on her thoughtlessness, and on the duty of trying. After waiting nearly quarter of an hour for the boys, who seemed not to have heard the clock strike, Mr. Alcott began to read without them. He said he should not read one journal, it was so badly written. He began another, during which time the absent boys came in, having stayed out twenty minutes too long.

At the commencement of the school, Mr. Alcott appointed the recess at half-past eleven, that the clock striking twelve might be the signal for return; and this he distinctly said to each scholar, as they were sent out, one by one, for their first recess. A lady, who came to place her son at school that day, expressed her astonishment at Mr. Alcott's confidence in such little boys' obedience, and said she was very sure her boy would not come in, if he were among them. When her boy came to school some weeks after, it is true that he did play truant frequently, not only at recess-time, but before school, and, in one or two instances, did not come to school at all. But none of the other scholars ever remained out five minutes after the clock struck, excepting, in one instance, a very imaginative boy from the country, who had just entered the school, wandered to the other side of the Common, with a little fellow of five years, and in this instance of to-day, when the boys declared that they did not hear the clock strike, being in Temple Court, instead of on the mall. Mr. Alcott, having entire confidence in their word, merely told them not to play in the court another day, at least without a sentinel to watch the clock.

February 2d. — Mr. Alcott made remarks upon journal writing, to the older boys, and upon the desirableness of education to those who were to wield the interests of the world by commerce. He came to a little boy, and said, Oh! I am very much encouraged about you; you have written a whole column of words; you begin to know what you are in school for.

He then took Krummacher, to read a parable to the little class. He read the story of the Canary-bird, talking with them, in his indescribable way, all the while.

After this, he took the younger division of the spelling class, and heard them pronounce their lessons in spelling, and told them the meanings of the words.

He told the rest of the class who had not broken any rule to turn round. All turned but two. Do any of you remember those words, "Set a watch upon thy heart"? Yes, said they. It does not mean to put a time-piece on your bodily heart, but to superintend your minds: have you put a sentinel over yourself to-day? What is the sentinel of the soul? Conscience. If the sentinel sleeps, what becomes of the city? The enemies get in, said a little boy. What is the enemy? said Mr. Alcott. Error, said one; Doubt, said another; Passion, said a third; Revenge, said another; Self-will, said several. In one word, Wickedness, said Mr. Alcott. Now all those who do not set a watch on themselves, I shall consider as not desiring to be better. Do you remember these words in the Bible: "By patient continuance in well-doing, seek"—for what? I don't remember, said the boy addressed. "Seek for glory, honor, and immortality," said a girl. How many of you have this patient continuance? None spoke.

Mr. Alcott remarked that one boy of this school had said, when asked why he did not answer Mr. Alcott's questions, Do you think I am going to speak before thirty children? As many of you as have this feeling of embarrassment may hold up their hands. Several held up their hands; and he spoke of the duty of making an effort to conquer this feeling, since it was impossible for him to assist them in cultivating their minds, unless they would show him the state of them. He then asked them to spell the words, which they did.

The word *birch* led them to the consideration of school discipline. And they all spontaneously said that they had never been in a school where there was so much order, and so little punishment, as in this. Mr. Alcott asked them how they felt when he punished them; and they said that they always felt he punished them for their own good, and not from anger.

Something was said of hurting the body, as a means of reaching the mind; and that, in some instances, boys needed bodily punishment to rouse their sluggishness of mind, because they would not attend to the meanings of words, and could not be reached by words that were intended to revive the conscience. Other boys needed it on account of their obstinacy and opposition. There were rivers which were very strong, but would not go in the channel made for them by God, but wanted to make new channels; and there were some stagnant waters, and some shallow rivers which babbled. As he described these various rivers, the boys appropriated to themselves and one another the various types; and Mr. Alcott confirmed some of these, as very just applications.

February 3d. — I did not come to school; but when a little boy, who lived in the house with me, came home, he told me they wrote till ten o'clock. And then Mr. Alcott read about Christian, — how he came to the Cross, and his burden fell off into the sepulchre; and he said Mr. Alcott told of a procession, and proposed that they should all go in it, and bury their bad habits, — the bundles on their backs. (Mr. Alcott told me, this morning, that the subject of self-sacrifice was discussed, when he brought Christian to the foot of the cross; and it was under this principle of self-surrender that the imaginary procession was formed.)

The little boy also told me that, after recess, Mr. Alcott described two words, and that the boys said one was heaven, and one was hell. (Mr. Alcott said that he described the world of spirit and the world of flesh, and the issues of these different principles, in an allegory; and that the children themselves came to the conclusions, and alone used those words.) This little boy also told me that Mr. Alcott said he could tell what shapes their minds would come forth in, if they could take shape; and, said he, mine came out in the very thing that I have always wanted more than any thing else; and he screamed with laughter, as he exclaimed, The very, very thing! Well, what was it? said his mother and I at the same moment. A sword, said he, — a sword to prick all the boys with! Can you remember the shape that any other soul came forth in? said I. He said two of the boys were to come forth as whispers; but he did not remember the rest.

February 4th. — I arrived at quarter-past nine, and found them all writing their journals or their spelling lessons. At quarter of ten, Mr. Alcott began to read to the younger division of the spelling class, and to those of the youngest class who were present. He read a parable of Krummacher to illustrate Indolence, which not only awakened their attention very strongly, but attracted the notice of many of the rest; and he talked a little with a boy of the larger class, to enforce the lesson upon him.

At ten o'clock, the class turned to spell. They all spelled well, until it came to one little boy, who missed. Mr. Alcott said, Do you know why you do not spell the words right? The child looked inquiringly. It is because you do not use your eyes to see how the letters are placed; and so you have no picture of the word in your mind. And he went on describing how he should look at the letters, picture them out, lay up the picture in his mind, and, when he heard the word, should think how one letter came after the other. He talked a great while; and not only the one addressed, but all the little boys, seemed much interested and edified. The words were defined to these children, and then Mr. Alcott called the rest of the class to turn and spell.

Birth was the first word. Mr. Alcott remarked that we had once before talked of birth, and their ideas had been brought out. Now I am going to speak of it again, and we shall read Wordsworth's ode. He then asked the youngest child present how old he was, and found he was four. The oldest was twelve. He said, That little boy, in four years, has not had time to make that comparison of thoughts and feelings which makes up conscious life. He asked those who understood him to hold up their hands. Several held up their hands. Those who do not understand these words may hold up their hands. A great many of the younger ones held up their hands.

I am not surprised that you did not understand; but perhaps you will understand some things I am going to say. Do you feel, said he to the oldest, that any change has taken place in you in twelve years? do things seem the same to you as they did six years ago? She recognized a change. A boy of ten said that he did also. Wordsworth had lived, when he wrote this ode, many years, and consequently had felt changes, and he expresses this in the lines I am about to read. He then began and read the first stanza:—

There was a time when meadow, grove, and stream,
The earth and every common sight,
To me did seem
Apparelled in celestial light,
The glory and the freshness of a dream.
It is not now as it has been of yore;
Turn wheresoe'er I may,
By night or day,
The things which I have seen I now can see no more

He here stopped, and asked why Wordsworth could not see the things which he had seen before; had they changed, or had he changed? He had changed, said a boy of ten. Have you had any degree of this change? Yes, and more in this last year than in all my life before.

He then said, But let us all look back six months; how many of you look at things, and feel about them, differently from what you did six months ago? How many of you feel that this school-room is a different place from what it was the first week you were here? Almost every one immediately, with great animation, held up his hand. He then asked those who knew why this was, to hold up their hands. Many did. And when called on to answer, they severally said, Because we know more, because we think more, because we understand you, because you know us, because you have looked inside of us. Mr. Alcott said, The place is very different to me; and why? They gave similar answers; but he said they had not hit it. At last one said, Because we behave better. Yes, said he, you have it now; knowledge is chaff of itself; but you have taken the knowledge and used it to govern yourselves, and to make yourselves better. If I thought I gave you knowledge only, and could not lead you to use it to make yourselves better, I would never enter this school-room again.

He went on and read the next stanza of the ode: —

> The rainbow comes and goes,
> And lovely is the rose,
> The moon doth with delight
> Look round her when the heavens are bare.
> Waters on a starry night
> Are beautiful and fair.
> The sunshine is a glorious birth;
> But yet I know, where'er I go,
> That there hath passed away a glory from the earth; —

stopping to ask them about the effects of the rainbow, the rose, the waters on a starry night, on themselves; remarking, There are some minds which live in the world, and yet are insensible; which do not see any beauty in the rainbow, the moon, the waters on a starry night. As he went on through the next stanza, so descriptive of the animation and beauty of spring, he paused on every line, and asked questions. Why are "the cataracts said to blow their trumpets"? A little girl said, Because the waters dash against the rocks. "The echoes thronging through the woods" led out to recollections of the sound in the woods in spring; to echoes which they had severally heard. As the animating pictures of "children pulling flowers on May-day," the "child springing up on the mother's arm," &c., came up, every countenance expressed the most vivid delight; and one girl exclaimed, What a succession of beautiful pictures! All full of life, said Mr. Alcott; and he went on:—

> But there's a tree of many one,
> A single field which I have looked upon;
> Both of them speak of something that is gone:
> The pansy at my feet
> Doth the same tale repeat:
> Whither is fled the visionary gleam?
> Where is it now, the glory and the dream?

When he had read these lines, he said, Was that a thought of life? No, a thought of death, said several. Yes, said Mr. Alcott, Wordsworth had lived long enough to feel changes: he had known death, as well as life. He then went on —

> Our birth is but a sleep and a forgetting, —

and stopped and asked how that was. After a pause, one of the most intelligent boys, eight years old, said he could not imagine. The two oldest girls said they understood it, but could not explain it in words. Do you understand it? said Mr. Alcott to a little boy of five who was holding up his hand. Yes. Well, what does it mean? Why, you know, said he very deliberately, that, for all that our life seems so long to us, it is a very short time to God; and so when we die it seems all a sleep to God. He repeated this at Mr. Alcott's request, and I said to him, So Mr. Wordsworth was thinking of God, and how God felt, on seeing that a child was born into the world? He paused, looked a little confused, and repeated the word *forgetting*. I said, Wait, and tell me your thought. Why, you know, said he, God knows us, but we don't. He looked at me with a look of doubt, whether I should understand him. And our knowledge of ourselves, in comparison with what God knows about us, said I, seems like forgetfulness itself? Yes, said he, that is it (with a cleared up countenance). All the rest listened with interest and an expression of great pleasure; and then one girl said, The soul comes from heaven; it goes to sleep in that world, and wakes up in this. Mr. Alcott then read on to the line —

Heaven lies about us in our infancy,

when he shut up the book, and asked every child separately what he understood by birth. They all answered; and many repeated the definitions which they gave the other day. When they had answered all round, Mr. Alcott observed that there was one striking difference in their answers; some expressed the idea that the soul shaped and made the body; others that the body was made, and the soul put into it. Which is right? said one boy. That is more than I can tell, but I incline to the first opinion. You are all nearly right, however; you have the important ideas; birth is not the beginning of the spirit; life is the remembrance, or a waking up of spirit. All the life of knowledge is the waking up of what is already within, —

The rising of life's star, that had elsewhere its setting.

What is life's star? The soul, said they. But birth is sometimes the prelude to the death of the soul, said Mr. Alcott. How? said one boy. Because the soul becomes the slave of the body; is governed, darkened, shut up, and buried in it; and it is necessary that it should be born again, born out of the body; do you understand that? Yes. Some of you have needed to be born again into your new life, said Mr. Alcott. Then he asked, Do you know what *pulp* means? Several said, Yes. Mr. Alcott continued, It is the part of the fruit round the seed; and its use is to cherish the seed, and give it life, and make it fit to become the beginning of a new tree or plant. Well, do you understand my figure when I say, that the body is a pulp, and that its use is to cherish and protect the spiritual seed? Many of them said, Yes. Well, suppose that we take the seed of a plant, and put it in the ground; what happens to it? They were silent, and he added: It bursts, and some parts shoot down into the earth, and some parts shoot up towards the light. Now can you understand this, — that *the soul* is a seed placed in the midst of the world, represented by the ground; and that the shoots which go down into the earth, to fasten the plant in the earth awhile, are the bodily feelings and appetites; — and that the shoots which go upward towards the light, are the affections and better feelings that seek Heaven? They said, Yes. Well, suppose that more of the seed shoots downward than is necessary; and that no shoots go upward; would there be any flower and fruit? No. It would all be *root;* all would be under the earth. Well, can you understand that if the soul loves the body only, and only uses its animal appetites, and does not seek the light and Heaven, it will have no beauty nor fruit; but will be an earthly, dark thing, a root? Yes, they understood that. Well, said he, now you know why I wish to check your animal appetites; your love of the body, when that interferes with the mind's growth. It is right to love your body in a degree; — the body has its uses; but it is one thing to take care of your body and another to indulge it. The plant must have root enough to make it stand steady in the earth; but that is enough.

February 5th. — I arrived at half-past nine, and found the children in their seats. Mr. Alcott talked a little with the little commentator of yesterday, commending him for his writing, and especially because he had been rather indocile, not through opposition, but from a sort of obstinate clinging to his own inward thoughts, which are probably clearer than those of most children of his age.

Mr. Alcott read from Northcotes' Fables to the little class, and had a long talk with them on Punishment, to make them comprehend its theory, the hurting of the body for the benefit of the mind; and their faces looked all "like fires new stirred," as they listened. I thought I should like to have some of those skeptics who do not believe children can comprehend the sacrifice of the body to the mind, to have seen these little things, under four years of age, listen to and apprehend the philosophy of pain.

At ten the whole school turned to face Mr. Alcott; and he then arranged some restless boys in situations where he thought they would not be tempted. A great deal of talk was made about these arrangements, in order to impress them with the great importance of complete self-control. Mr. Alcott said that, if interrupted to-day, he should discontinue his readings.

He then read the first stanzas of the "Castle of Indolence," without letting them know what it was, and asked each to write on his slate what he thought it represented. They severally wrote: Sluggishness — Calm Pleasures — Sleep — Ease — Heaven — Doubt — Death — Earth — The World — and Deception. Mr. Alcott having gone round, and looked at each, told them each to keep their own secret; and he read it again. Several changed their opinions, and there were added new answers: Idleness — Pleasures — Sleepiness — Solitude — Laziness — Silence — Deceit — Misers — Slumber — Hell — Doubting Castle — and several said Indolence.

Mr. Alcott then read the "Song of the Wizard," and asked, who believed, with the wizard, that hard work makes all the vice in the world. A large, lazy boy held up his hand; but a little boy of six made a gesture of astonishment at his doing so. When Mr. Alcott read the Invitation, he asked who would accept it? Some smiled and held up their hands. He read through the description of the interior of the castle, and the Mirror of Vanity; and when he stopped, said, As many of you as think you ever visited this castle, hold up your hands. Thirteen held up their hands. How many of you delight to rise at break of day, cold mornings? Almost all held up their hands. This room, he continued, is often the Castle of Indolence; and he pointed to several chairs, saying of each, That is a Castle of Indolence.

After recess, the younger children found their arithmetic all prepared for them. The rest found their Commonplace Books in their places; and "The American Flag" was selected, by one of the boys, for the lesson. Mr. Alcott asked him to read the part he liked best, and he read the stanzas following: —

Flag of the brave, thy folds shall fly,
The sign of hope and triumph, high.
When speaks the signal trumpet-tone,
And the long line comes gleaming on,
(Ere yet the life-blood, warm and wet,
Has dimmed the glistening bayonet,)
Each soldier's eye shall brightly turn
To where thy meteor glories burn,
And, as his springing steps advance,
Catch war and vengeance from the glance;

And, when the cannon-mouthings loud
Heave, in wild wreaths, the battle shroud,
And gory sabres rise and fall,
Like shoots of flame on midnight's pall,
There shall thy victor-glances glow,
And cowering foes shall sink beneath
Each gallant arm that strikes below
That lovely messenger of death.

Flag of the seas, on ocean's wave
Thy stars shall glitter o'er the brave.
When death, careering on the gale,
Sweeps darkly round the bellied sail,
And frightened waves rush wildly back
Before the broadside's reeling rack,
The dying wanderer of the sea
Shall look at once to heaven and thee,
And smile to see thy splendors fly
In triumph o'er his closing eye.

Flag of the free heart's only home,
By angel-hands to valor given,
Thy stars have lit the welkin dome,
And all thy hues were born in heaven.
Forever float that standard sheet!
Where breathes the foe, but falls before us,
With Freedom's soil beneath our feet,
And Freedom's banner streaming o'er us?

When he had read these stanzas, Mr. Alcott asked one of the rest if he knew why that boy liked those stanzas so much. The boy addressed said it was because he had such a temper, he liked to have things in his own way. Another said, because he liked battling and violence. The boy himself said it was because he liked his country; and he read over again the most warlike lines of the piece. The girls all laughed as he read the words "war and vengeance" with so much gusto. Mr. Alcott said, Well, he is very ingenuous; he turns out himself before us; he loves vengeance, war, slaughter, don't he? Yes, said he. Do you ever think of the sufferers? Sometimes I think of the widows. Which do you think of most, the soldiers or the widows? About the same. I am sorry; but I hope you will think of the widows most, by and by. Mr. Alcott then read the same stanzas very slowly, and stopped and asked questions about every line. What is the image here? What feeling does it gratify? One boy said, Did you hear Dr. Channing's sermon,* sir? No; but I know what he thinks. I am glad you remember it. A little girl said, I did not hear it! (very despondingly.) Mr. Alcott then spoke of the right of self-defence and of defensive war; and there was quite a discussion, which resulted, I thought, in very just views all round. One boy, on being asked, said there was nothing in the piece which pictured out any of his thoughts and feelings. But at last he read the last stanza, as the one he liked best on the whole.

Mr. Alcott then asked, What is freedom? does it give us the right to do as we please? No. What is it? the opportunity for what? He did not know. Is it the right to do right, or to do either right or wrong? To do right. The boy who had selected the piece said it was, besides, the right to speak one's own mind. Mr. Alcott said, What! carelessly, whether it will do good or harm? At first he said, Yes; then, No. An-

* Sermon on War.

other boy said, We have no right to do as we please, unless we please to do right. The girls agreed with him. Mr. Alcott then told the boy who had selected the piece that his difficulties at home and at school arose from his confounding the ideas of freedom and indulgence. He then spoke of law as the guardian of freedom, and the laws of this school as emanating from conscience.

One boy, on being asked which stanza he liked best, said he saw very little in the whole thing; he never wanted to be a soldier. The boy who had selected the piece said he wanted to be a soldier; he wanted to ride on horseback, and be dressed up in uniform. It would not be so pleasant to ride unless he could be dressed up in uniform. Another boy wanted to be a king. As this ode hardly admitted of a paraphrase, having few ideas in it, or the little charm they had being in the words, Mr. Alcott said they might go and write their journals while he heard the arithmetic lessons.

February 6th. — I arrived at half past nine, and found them at their spelling lessons, as usual. Immediately Mr. Alcott commenced with the youngest class, and read about Frank's breaking the window. He made a very animated lesson on ingenuousness, by a conversation intermingled with the reading; which, as usual, led them to the conclusion that they should prefer punishment to going on in wrong-doing.

This is the great principle which Mr. Alcott labors to bring out in the young consciousness, to be willing to be punished, to accept punishment, in order that they may not indulge themselves in wrong-doing, and to look upon pain as the instrument of producing good character. His own little girl is led to tell him of the naughty things she does; and the telling does not save her from chastisement, but often only ensures it. Even the scholars here often tell him what will produce punishment, knowing that their ingenuousness does not save them from the penalty, so successful has he been in making them feel that spiritual good is worth deprivation, or bodily pain, or whatever the punishment may be.

Mr. Alcott then took the youngest class but one, and heard them spell their lesson, giving a great deal of time to that little boy whose deep interest in the general makes it a peculiar effort for him to enter into the details of the particular. It is really very curious to see, on the one hand, how difficult it is for this child to receive a strong impression from any outward arbitrary thing, like a letter, or the arrangement of letters; and, on the other hand, how rapidly and completely his mind discovers the idea conveyed by a poetical image or a natural fact. Nature seems transparent to his eye; but it is for him an effort of abstraction to see the outward and arbitrary.

The lesson was spelled, and the younger division were asked if they received new ideas while we talked about the words. After a while, one after another held up their hands. One little boy said he understood Mr. Alcott when he spoke to himself, but not always when he talked to others. Mr. Alcott asked him whose words he understood best. He said, Mother's and father's and Mr. Alcott's. Mr. Alcott said, Do we all talk about the same things? No, said he; mother talks about things out, and you about things inside; and he touched his head to express the inside.

Mr. Alcott then said, I am thinking of a dreadful law. What if all boys found in a lazy position, with things in their hands, or inattentive, were to receive a blow upon the hand? A large boy said that would not be just. Mr. Alcott asked him if it was not just that he should punish a certain boy (naming him), if he did what would interfere with his own attention and the attention of others. Yes, but not so. Mr. Alcott asked if he had not a right to choose his own modes of reaching the mind; and when words did not do, and a slight pain on the body did do, if he had not a right, if it was not his duty, to take that means. The boy said, Any other way but that. Mr. Alcott asked the rest if they thought it would be just to punish them as he proposed, if they did what he had spoken of, and indulged themselves in these habits after so much instruction as they had had. Every one held up his hand but this boy, who has a horror of physical pain, which is peculiar. I said to him, I cannot conceive why you should think that it is so dreadful to have a touch of pain on your body, that you can one moment weigh with it your improvement of mind; I should prefer to be beaten like a West Indian slave to resting in a bad habit. One of the girls said, I should be very glad to be whipped, if it would cure me of my bad habits. Mr. Alcott asked those who would willingly receive a good deal of bodily pain from him if it would rid them of these habits of inattention and self-indulgence, which interfere with us every day, to hold up their hands. All, except one little boy and the great boy spoken of before, held up hands.

The uses of pain, in developing the mind and awakening sympathy, were considered; and a comparison of the external and internal world was made. And Mr. Alcott said his little girl came to him, the other day, and said that her sister had pulled her hair and pinched her cheek. Now, her sister was a boisterous child, who inflicted pain thoughtlessly; and he called the little girl (knowing that it was as Anna had said) and said, "Sister says you pulled her hair so (and he gave her a hard pull), and that you pinched her cheek so" (and he gave her a hard pinch, but did not look at her any differently from usual). He said that she immediately understood how her sister had been hurt; and sympathy arose in her mind; and she spontaneously went and kissed her. Do you think it was worth while that I should give her pain, to bring out that sympathy, or let her mind go uncultivated, because I was afraid of hurting her body? The result of the conversation seemed to be a universal agreement with Mr. Alcott.

The first interesting word that was illustrated to-day was *bleed*. One boy said, The heart bleeds when it has suffering. Mr. Alcott said that these figurative, or rather he would say spiritual meanings, were the most real; the literal meaning was the real meaning in things; but nothing happened in things which did not image forth some movement of spiritual life.

The word *blend* was variously illustrated and defined. One little boy of five years old said, When a thing is made of one substance, and when we want it to be of a different color, some other substance is put over, and then the two are said to be blended. Mr. Alcott said, This boy's definitions are from his own mint; and then he explained this figure, by describing a mint.

Blind led to the idea of spiritual blindness. Mr. Alcott said, Some of you, when you first came to this school, were spiritually blind; some are here now who are spiritually blind; their outward eye is a very good one, but they do not seem to look inward. The spiritual eye is the soul itself; and he quoted Byron's words: "A thing of eyes," &c. He spoke of the causes of spiritual blindness. He said the reason that boy with whom he had just been talking could not understand the theory of punishment was because his soul was blinded by the predominance of bodily fear, and outward things occupied his thoughts.

A great deal was said about the uses of the bodily eye; the cultivation of it connected with a parallel advancement of spiritual vision; and the reciprocal influences of bodily and spiritual vision on each other, and on the advancement of the mind and soul.

At last he called for the slates of the superintendents, for there had been two. On one there was only the superintendent's own name; the other had several names, which were explained; and the boy had evidently been very careful to do justice. None thought he had been unjust. Mr. Alcott said what was set down did not warrant any punishment; they had all tried, and had succeeded in being self-controlled and attentive. Before he said this, however, and while they were expecting punishment, a little boy said, I spoke, but he has not written me down. Mr. Alcott said, You are right to tell me.

After recess, I took my scholars into the other room. When they came back, Mr. Alcott asked who had been faulty; and several held up their hands. Mr. Alcott asked one of these what he had done. Played. Why? He did not know. At last he said he was thoughtless. Why? He did not know.

Mr. Alcott took him from his seat, and led him to the little boy who gives such spiritual answers, and said, Ask that little boy how you can learn to think? The little boy said, with his usual slow enunciation, and self-involved look, Oh! he must employ all his thoughts. Well, said Mr. Alcott, that is very good advice. But I don't know how, said the boy. He doesn't know how, said Mr. Alcott to the child, who replied with a great effort to get out the words, Why, then he must set his heart to work. Very well, said Mr. Alcott; you must set your heart to work, and employ all your thoughts; and then you will not play when you ought to be doing something else.

I found Mr. Alcott had given a writing lesson on the

black tablets to the rest of the school, while I had had my Latin class in the other room.

February 7th. — I came and looked over my Journal before the reading commenced, as it is to be read after recess.

Now, said Mr. Alcott, I am going to ask all a question, of which you must think before you answer. What do you love best? God! said the first one addressed, without any hesitation. Mr. Alcott said, I should like a more deliberate and particular answer, and I will put the question in another form. Do you love any being or thing as well as yourself? Yes, said he. Do you love any being or thing better than yourself? I do not know. The next said he thought he loved God best, better than his mother, better than himself. All the most thoughtless boys were very sure they loved God best; and also one or two of the most thoughtful. One little boy at first could not tell. At last he said he thought it was his mother. Another little boy said he loved his uncle Charles best. Why? He did not want to tell. Do you love him because he is good, or because he loves you, or because he has given you any thing? Because he is good. Did he ever give you any thing? Yes. Has he given you any thing lately? No, he is in England. The next little boy said he loved God best, Jesus Christ next, and his mother next. Why do you love your mother? Because she takes care of me. Why do you love Jesus Christ? Because he is holy. [Mr. Alcott did not hear, and the second time he said, Because he is good.]

Why do you love God? Because he is good. Do you love yourself? Not one grain. Don't you love your mind? That is not myself. What is yourself? My body. Don't you love it? No. Don't you love to feed it? Yes! said he, slowly, with surprise at this home question. Do you love to feed it more than you ought to do? Yes, said he, with a sigh, and a look of deep reflection.

There were no more new ideas given. I intimated that I thought many had answered as if the question was, What ought you to love best? which produced a few remarks from Mr. Alcott.

February 12*th.*—Mr. Alcott read from Krummacher, "The Birth of the Caterpillar."

What is in your mind? said he, to a boy of eight years old, as soon as he had finished. I cannot express it, he replied. Is it a thought, or a feeling? Both: it is a belief. What have you learned from this story? said Mr. Alcott to another boy of the same age. It reminds me that when the body dies, the soul will live, and go to heaven. How long have you had that thought? Ever since I was four years old. Do you remember the time when you did not have it? Yes, when I was very little, I thought we did not live after our bodies died. Another boy of the same age said he never remembered the time when he did not believe in life's going on. Do all believe without a shadow of doubt that they shall live after death has taken place? I believe it, said a boy of nine, but not without a shadow of doubt. A boy of six said, When we die, an angel comes from heaven, and takes us, — the shell and all. What is the shell? said Mr. Alcott. The body, said another child of the same age. Do you want to stay in your bodies awhile? Yes, said both, with a smile. What did you think while I was reading this story? said Mr. Alcott to a thoughtful little boy of five. I thought God changed the caterpillar into a butterfly, and then there was an angel that went in, and ascended into heaven, and when it got to heaven the butterfly's body fell again to the earth. But where did the butterfly come from? God changed the caterpillar into a butterfly; the body of the caterpillar was changed into the form of a butterfly. Who made the caterpillar? God. What did God make it of? He made it out of dust. Nothing but dust? Nothing but dust. When did the angel go into the butterfly? When it began to move. Where did the angel come from? I did not think, — I must stop to think, said he. In a minute he went on. The angel must have been in the worm, — some of it. Where did the angel come from? God sent it. Did the angel help to make the caterpillar into a butterfly? No; but God made the body of the caterpillar into the body of a butterfly, and covered over the angel with it. You see it was not a real butterfly, but it seemed so to the eyes. It was made to carry the angel up to heaven with its wings. Do you think every butterfly has an angel in it, like that one? Oh, no! Well, how came it to be so, that particular time? Why, God wanted to show Adam and all of them an angel going to heaven, and he could not do it without something for their eyes. Why did he want to show them an angel going to heaven? Oh! so that they need not mourn any longer for their brother Abel. I think, said I, that God means to put us in mind of the soul's going to heaven by every butterfly that he makes. *Do you?* said he very slowly, his thoughtful countenance lighting up into a bright smile. (Is not that a mind in the kingdom? said Mr. Alcott to me, after this conversation was over.) What does this story bring to your mind? said he to a girl of twelve. The life of the senses, the change of death, and immortality. In the Bible some one says, *I die daily:* do you understand that? Yes: it means you daily go more and more away from the senses, into the inward life.

And here I will give the record that I made of one of the reading lessons of the first class. It was "An address to a dying child," in the Commonplace Book of Poetry, and selected by one of the class, eight years old, who began with reading it all through.

Which verse do you like best? said Mr. Alcott. The boy read, —

> Yes, thou art going home,
> Our Father's face to see.

I like those lines very much. Why? What sentiment do they awaken? The pleasure of seeing God; dying and going up to stay with God. Have you never seen God here? Yes, in one way; but I like to think of dying and going up to God. Which way do you suppose is *up?* *Up* is by the sun, — higher than the sun.

Do the people on the other side of this round earth say *up?* This led to considerations on the illusions of the senses, and what that idea was which was signified by this emblem of place. The idea seemed to be gained; and the boy paraphrased the lines thus: —

> You are going within yourself,
> Your Father's face to see through your own spirit.

Do you know, said Mr. Alcott, you never would have seen the outward world, except by first going within yourself? After a long pause of thought, the boy replied, Yes, I see how it is. Why is it said, Father's *face?* I don't know why they say *face.* What do you see in any person's face? The mind, the expression of the soul, said he, after some hesitation. And if God expresses himself in any way to us, when we go inward, and think over our own faculties and feelings, which are his expressions of love to us, is it not very natural to say we have seen his *face?* Yes. I cannot help thinking God has a real face, said another boy of the same age. Can you think of your own spirit without thinking of a face? Yes. Then why not of God's spirit? I can. Do you think you see more of your brother, when you see his body with your eyes, or think about him in your mind? said Mr. Alcott to the reader. I realize him when I think of him, sometimes more than when I am looking at him.

Each of the class then read the verse that they liked best. One boy, who had been punished considerably since he came to school, read the verse beginning, —

O Father of our spirits,
We can but look to thee;
Though chastened, not forsaken,
Shall we thy children be, &c.

What is meant by chastened? said Mr. Alcott. Punished, disciplined. Can one be punished and not forsaken? Yes. Did you not think, when I first punished you, that I hated you? Yes. You thought I forsook you? Yes. Do you think so now? I have not thought so for a great while. You understand now that it was just the contrary of forsaking and hating you, to punish you? Yes. It was you that forsook me, and not I that forsook you? Yes. Read the last two lines.

Teach us to say, with Jesus,
Thy will, not ours, be done.

What do these lines express? Self-sacrifice, self-surrender. One of the girls read the third verse as the most beautiful.

Soon shall thy bright young spirit
From earth's cold chains be free, &c

What does it express? Liberty, said one. Blessedness, said several. What was the leading idea of the first verse? The expression of the eye; the appearances of death; it is descriptive; picturesque, — were the several answers. What is the idea of the second verse? The pains and pleasures of this earth, said one. Cannot you express it in one word? This life, said he, after a pause. What is the object of this life? said Mr. Alcott. To make us better; to try us. Oh! the idea of this verse is the trials of life. What is the idea of the fourth verse? It compares heaven and earth, said one. What of the last? Devotion, faith, said a boy of ten. Well, said Mr. Alcott. Death, human life, heaven, a comparison of the two, and the principle by which we rise from the human to the heavenly life, — this is a beautiful range of thought, is it not? Beautiful, said several. They were then sent to their seats to write a paraphrase.

III.

SELF-ANALYSIS.

I HAVE now given about five weeks of the Journal. But before quite dismissing it, I will give some farther extracts, comprising a weekly exercise, which was suggested by the following conversation, on the 9th of February.

The word *bless* came up among the words of the spelling lesson. It was defined as wishing well to others; wishing God's blessing; making happy. Mr. Alcott asked if any one felt he comprehended all its meaning. No hands were raised, and a small boy said, Mr. Alcott, I do not believe you comprehend all its meaning yourself. Mr. Alcott asked what blessings God gives. They answered severally, food, sun, air, clothing, dwellings, flowers, wisdom, our souls, parents. Do we have blessings whether we deserve them or not? Some said, Yes; some said, No. But there is one blessing greater than all you have mentioned. They severally answered, after some consideration, Spirit; God's Spirit; the Bible.

The Bible, said Mr. Alcott, is God in words. But the Bible is not the only Revelation of God. There are many Bibles, to those who think. Nature, the outward world, is a Bible. Its objects typify God's thoughts. The soul is a Bible. What do we read in the passions? I will tell you: God's punishments; for the passions are the over-mastering effects of indulgence. What tremendous pains they involve, by necessity!

But what blessings have you had? He addressed a boy, who thinks little, but who catches the habit of answering. He replied, The Bible. How is that a blessing? said Mr. Alcott. The Lord blesses us with it, said he. In what way? He makes us happy. With the Bible? He makes us good. Your answers do not sound as if they were your own reflections, but like parrotry. Tell me what blessings you have been blessed with to-day. With a mind. Are you thoughtless? said I (referring to a confession or excuse he always makes, when he has done wrong). Yes. But does not thoughtless mean without thoughts? Yes. Can there be a mind without thoughts? No. Then how can you say your mind is a blessing to you? I have been baptized, said he. How is that a blessing? It purified me. Are you pure, purified? I was for a little while after I was baptized. Was your soul or your body baptized? My body. Does not purity belong to the mind? Yes. Do truth and love keep the mind pure? Do you understand what I mean, when I say, the soul is baptized with truth and love? Yes. Was your soul ever baptized so? Yes. How often? Every day. How long does it last? A little while.

All these answers seemed given without thought; and Mr. Alcott pursued it still farther, his object being to show this fancifully worded boy that he had no self-knowledge; and that his ideas were not representations of his own thoughts and feelings, but mere verbal associations and meaningless images. This boy's memory of words and images, which has been over-cultivated, is great; and he seems to have been led into a shallow activity of mind and tongue, that deceives himself. I thought he was enlightened a little to-day; and the rest of the scholars, who were very attentive, and occasionally joined in the conversation with much intelligence, evidently understood his mind very well, and were guarded against the same fallacy.

Mr. Alcott here opened the Bible, and read the beatitudes in paraphrase, thus: —

Blessed, inconceivably happy, are those who feel as if they were without any thing; for such are prepared to receive heaven.

Blessed are they that mourn; for comfort comes to the mourner that others cannot understand.

Blessed are they that desire goodness more than any thing else; for they shall be filled with it.

Blessed are they that are kind and merciful; for they will not be in danger of being cruelly treated.

Blessed are those who are pure, and have no wrong affections or false thoughts; for they see God, his goodness, excellence, love, and truth.

Blessed are they who suffer in order to do right; for they already have heaven.

We began with our own definitions of *bless*, said he; and now you have heard Jesus Christ's definitions: do you understand, now, what *bless*, *blessed*, means? They all held up their hands.

When they returned to the school-room after recess, Mr. Alcott said, Such of you as gained some clearer ideas than you had before of one boy's mind this morning, hold up your hands. The older ones all did. Mr. Alcott here explained the difference between fancy and imagination, and asked which principle was in greatest activity in the mind of that boy. They replied, Fancy. What boy has an opposite kind of mind? Several were named. One of them, Mr. Alcott said, was literal. Two of them, he also said, had a very high degree of imagination. One had fancy and imagination also. Some farther questions were asked, which proved how truly children analyze each other's minds, when brought to attend to them; and it occurred to Mr. Alcott that there might be a regular lesson, the object of which would be to analyze individual characters, by means of certain testing questions: and this he carried into effect, although, practically, it became, instead of an analysis of individual character, an analysis of human nature in its more general point of view.

In pursuance of this plan, the next day Mr. Alcott arranged all the children in two semicircles around his blackboard, which was divided into compartments, thus: —

Spirit.	Soul.	Mind.
Love. | Faith. | Conscience.	Appetite. | Affection. Aspiration.	Imagination. | Judgment. Insight.
Good.	Happiness.	Truth.

Having explained the operations of Spirit, Soul, and Mind, after their respective objects, he asked the children what they thought he was going to do? They did not know. He asked who among them would be willing to be analyzed, and tell all their faults and virtues, for the benefit of themselves and the rest in self-knowledge. All held up their hands but one.

He then selected a little girl who was remarkably simple and truth-loving, and asked if she was willing to answer all his questions truly, whether they laid open her faults or her virtues. She replied, Yes; and all the rest expressed satisfaction.

LOVE.

Having drawn them into two concentric arcs of circles round his table, over which the blackboard hangs, Mr. Alcott began to speak of Love. Do you think you love? Yes. Whom? My mother. What do you love in your mother? She was silent. Her voice, her manners, her appearance, her spirit? Yes, all. Suppose she should lose her voice; and her appearance should change: should you still love her? Yes. You think that, independently of all that pleases your eye and mind, and of the good she does you,— even if she were to die, and you should see, hear, be taken care of by her no longer, you should still love her? Yes. What do the rest think? (These questions are not as many as were asked, however; the answers were very deliberate.) They all said, Yes, she does love, it is real love.

Mr. Alcott then said: If your mother were going to die, and the physicians said, If you would die, your mother's life could be saved, — would you die for your mother? She was silent. Mr. Alcott then went on to speak of the importance of her mother's life to her father, her brothers and sisters. She was still silent. How would it be with the rest? said he. One boy said, I should not hesitate one moment. Mr. Alcott inquired into this, and he said: Because his mother's life was more valuable to her friends than his was; because she was important to his younger brother, and because he should not be very happy in life if his mother were dead. There was some conversation with some other boys; and one said, that he was sure he could not die for his mother, though he cared more for her than for any one else. Mr. Alcott said, And what do you think you should lose if you died? He replied, I do not know. You would lose your body, said Mr. Alcott; and then turning to the little girl, he asked her if she had yet concluded whether she could die for her mother? Yes, said she very quietly, and after this long deliberation, in which it had been evident she endeavored not to deceive herself. Do the rest think she could? said Mr. Alcott. Yes, said several; I do not doubt she could. Well, said Mr. Alcott, do you think if by suffering a great deal of pain, you could make your father and mother happy all their lives, you would be willing to suffer? She was silent. Others cried out: Oh, yes! I know she could; and professed that they could. Mr. Alcott turned to the cast of

Christ, and spoke of his life; his sacrifice of enjoyment; his acceptance of suffering, his objects, his love. Questions were asked whose answers brought out a strong view of his spiritual, unselfish love of the spirits of men; and she was asked if she thought her love had any of this deep character. She was silent; and even the rest were here awed into some self-distrust. But few thought their love had any of the characteristics of Christ's love.

Mr. Alcott then asked her if she could bear the faults of others, and love them still? Sometimes. Can you bear with the impatience of your sisters and brothers at home? She smiled, and said she never had any occasion. Have you ever had occasion for forbearance and patience anywhere else? She did not remember, she said. Never in any instance; not in this school, nor anywhere? Yes, she recollected once; but not in this school. Well, did you forbear? Yes. Does any one else think this little girl has had occasion to forbear in this school? Several said, Yes. How many think she acted with forbearance? All held up their hands. Who think they have required her forbearance? Two held up their hands; and Mr. Alcott congratulated them on their acquisition of a better spirit than they had shown formerly.

Do you still think, said Mr. Alcott, that you really love,—love enough to sacrifice and forbear? Yes, said she. Nothing you have heard has led you to doubt this? No. What do the rest think? That she loves, she sacrifices, she forbears; that hers is real love.

Well, look at the scale. You see the first division is Spirit. The spirit comes from God; it loves, believes, obeys. We obey what we have faith in; we have faith in what we love; love is pure spiritual action. The spirit loves. The spirit, with its love, faith, and obedience, sanctifies or makes holy the soul, in its appetites, affections and aspirations, so that it gets happiness. And it clears and purifies the mind, in its faculties of insight, judgment, and imagination, so that it discovers truth.

FAITH.

Mr. Alcott began: We discovered last Wednesday that Love sacrifices and forbears. We might say a great deal more about love, but now we will go on to Faith. What is faith? Soon all the hands went up.

He began with the youngest, who said, Faith is spirit. Did you ever have any? Yes. The next said, Faith is not to doubt goodness in the spirits of people. Another said, Faith is a thought and feeling. When did you have faith? Yesterday. What was it about? I thought school kept yesterday afternoon; mother thought it did not; I was sure it did. Another said, Faith is only a feeling. Another said, Faith is love. There is faith in love, said Mr. Alcott. Another said, Faith is liking people from their looks. Whom have you faith in from her looks? I have faith in my mother. Why? Because I like her looks, and love her soul. All the children who had answered thus far were under six years old. One of seven years old said,

Faith is confidence in another. In another's what? In another's spirit; that people will do what they promise. A boy who is continually doing wrong, and failing in duty, said, Faith was obedience. Have you much faith? No. You have come pretty near losing your faith? Yes. Have you more now than you had some time ago? Yes. How will you get more faith? By doing as I am told. He looked serious, and somewhat distressed; and Mr. Alcott said, Well, go on and be obedient, and you will find faith. Another boy said, Faith is confidence. Whom have you confidence in? In you. Why? I don't know. A little girl said, Faith is to believe. Do you believe or doubt the most? I think I have more faith than doubt, said she. A boy said, Faith is to trust and believe. Is trust in the heart or head?. said Mr. Alcott. In the heart. And belief? In the head. Another boy said, To confide in the souls and promises of others. Another said, To confide in one you love. Then you must love? Yes. Faith then comes out of love? Yes, I think so.

One deaf boy, who sat near Mr. Alcott, but could not hear the rest speak, said: I don't know any thing about faith, but I guess I shall learn now. Then you already have some faith, said Mr. Alcott. Do you think faith is a thought or a feeling? They all decided that it was a feeling. Such of you as think this little girl has this feeling may hold up your hands. All did so. Such of you as have faith in her, faith that she will do as she promises, that she will not disappoint any just expectation, may hold up your hands. They all did so. Does any one doubt her? No one. Well, this is a matter of opinion; it is the head's faith. How many of you have the feeling, the faith that grows out of love to her? Several. Do you think that you have faith? said he, addressing her. Yes, I think I have. Can you remember any instance when you proved it? No. Do you generally think people are good when you first see them? Yes, generally; not always. In some particular instance that you have not had faith, can you tell what was the reason? I don't remember. Do you have faith in people's good intentions, even when you see that they do wrong? Yes, generally. Can you think of any persons in whom you have no faith; in whom you have no confidence? A very few. Do you think, as you grow older, that you have more or less faith in others? More in some people. Can you make a distinction between people in whose intentions you confide, and those in whose characters and actions you confide; have you been disappointed much? She thought not much.

How is it with the rest of you, — do any of you doubt more than confide and love? One boy held up his hand. Do you want to doubt? I cannot help it in many instances. Does the doubt come from your heart or head? I don't know. Several more doubters held up their hands, and were conversed with. Who of you think you believe more, and doubt less, than you did six months ago? Most held up their hands.

Mr. Alcott then turned to the little girl. In whom have you faith? In my father and mother. Has your faith more feeling than thought in it; or more thought than feeling? More feeling than thought. Do you think you get thoughts at this school which explain your feelings more and more? Yes: I think the mind explains the heart, said she. Knowledge explains faith? Yes. Does faith begin in feeling or thought? In feeling. Has a little infant any faith? Yes, a great deal. On this question, a boy whom I asked replied that he thought an infant brought faith into the world with it; for when it did mischief, it always thought that its mother could mend it all, and perhaps that was the reason it was so apt to do mischief. And was there not great profoundness in this observation? The unity of children's spiritual being is so deep and interior, that it is long before division, a break, or destruction, even in the outward world, can be apprehended. The natural condition of things in their apprehension is unity and perfection. In apparently disturbing this, they feel their own power. To reconstruct the unity of the spirit is Art, man's highest action, a dim image of the creativeness of God. Mr. Alcott went on: If all come into the world with faith in their hearts, what is the purpose of living here? Listen and hear what this little girl says. She said, To try to keep our faith. Yes, said Mr. Alcott, that is a great truth; you must try to keep it by feeling it out, thinking it out, and then acting it out.

What is the first object, out of itself, on which the faith of an infant rests? On its mother. What brings faith out of its spirit? The mother's love. Does it stop in the mother? No, it goes to the father, to the brothers and sisters. Does it stop there? No, it goes to God. Does it go immediately to God? Not till it hears about him, said she. Have you faith in any thing but persons? After a while she said she had faith in Nature. Have you faith in yourself? Yes. Your faith begins in yourself, and goes all round among your friends, and into Nature, till it finds God? Yes. Who gave you faith? God. God then is the source and supreme object of faith. Did you ever hear these words, "In him we live, and move, and have our being"? Yes; it is in the Bible. When did God give you faith? When he made my soul — it is my spirit. Yes, said Mr. Alcott; as a tree without sap would be no tree, but a dead thing, so a soul without faith would be no spirit. This little girl has faith in herself, in her soul, in her father, mother, sisters, friends, teachers; in Nature, and in God. One of the boys said, God should have come first. Mr. Alcott said, She means that she has found out her faith, and her knowledge of God has explained the feeling of faith entirely.

What is likely to carry faith away, or deaden it? There was no answer. He continued, Other parts of our nature, especially the appetites, may carry faith away, may quench the spirit. What tries your faith most? My impatience. All the rest seemed surprised and laughed; and declared that she never was impatient. Mr. Alcott said, If she calls herself impatient, what do you think of yourselves? This involved a long talk, in which the most impatient boy in school expressed it to be his opinion that he was very patient. He made out to prove that he was not utterly destitute of patience, that he was not always infinitely impatient. But, like most persons who think a great deal more about themselves than other people, he takes the germ that really exists for the cultivated plant which might but does not come from it. Mr. Alcott now turned to the little girl. Have you ever been impatient in this room? Yes. About your lessons? About my Latin lesson. (Her teacher can truly say it never was perceptible.) Have you ever felt impatient with any of the scholars? No, they treat me very kindly. Such as think that they have ever treated this little girl ungenerously, unkindly, may hold up their hands. Four or five did. Did you know it? said Mr. Alcott to her. No, said she.

Suppose some one should say about you (and he particularized many slanders), could you preserve your faith in people's good intentions, and in yourself, and in God? After a long silence she said, I should know my sisters would not believe it. You have too much faith to imagine such slanders? said Mr. Alcott. Another girl said, A good person could not be slandered so. Socrates was slandered so, said Mr. Alcott: he lost his life on the absurd accusation of having corrupted the youth of Athens. The martyrs were accused of bad intentions towards society. Jesus was accused of deceiving the people, on the one hand, and of wishing to dethrone Cæsar Augustus and become Emperor, on the other. There was never a great benefactor to man, who was not accused of being opposed to the very objects he had at heart. And it is often so in common life. The noble-souled are misunderstood. The generous are misrepresented. Martyrs, and even discoverers of science, have been uniformly traduced by people around them. The greatest benefactors of the present age are slandered. Some of the best people I know are the most slandered. Have you faith enough to bear slander then? for, if you have not, you will not keep your faith. She thought she had.

OBEDIENCE.

Mr. Alcott began: We have found that this little girl's love is so spiritual that it has in it self-sacrifice and forbearance; and she has faith enough in herself, her friends, in Nature, and in God, to give her courage and fortitude. You see, by the scale, that the Spirit not only loves and trusts, but obeys. Do you know what it is to obey? To follow. How? With actions. Must there be any feeling in the action? Yes, — a willing feeling. What should we obey? Reason and conscience, said a large boy. Is not reason always in conscience? No. What is there in conscience, when there is no reason? I cannot express it. Another boy said, We should obey the Bible and conscience. What is it within you to which the Bible speaks? The conscience, said he, at last. Some of the little ones said, We must obey the Ten Commandments; fathers and mothers; the Lord; and one said, Our own spirit. How do you find out, said Mr. Alcott to him, when you want to know what is right and what is wrong? I ask conscience. Another boy said, I ask my parents. A case was stated in which the parents could not be near; and it was asked, How should you do then? I don't know. Would not conscience tell you? If I knew which was right, conscience would tell me to do it. You must know first, then, before conscience would speak? Yes. (This boy was seven years old.)

Another boy then asked, If one's parents should tell me to kill somebody, would it be right to do it? What do you think? said Mr. Alcott. I think it would not be right, said he. Why? Because God commands us not to do wrong. You would know it was wrong then, even if your parents did not tell you so? Yes. Then you do not depend solely on your parents to know right from wrong? We know God's commandments, said he. Suppose you were in a country where the true God's commands were not known, but the laws of an imagined wicked god were the law of the land, as in some heathen countries: should you know it was wrong to murder? I think I should. Then conscience is not made up of what has been told you is right and wrong? Yes, it is. How, then, would it be made up in a country where the true God is not known? It would not be a good conscience; but there is some of the true God in everybody's conscience. (This boy was nine years old.) I hoped Mr. Alcott would tell him that this vision of the true God, which is in every conscience, more or less, is the spontaneous reason; and that the feeling which gives it authority is the sense of Absolute Being which we share with all spirits, even God. But he turned now to the little girl.

Do you think you have always obeyed? No, sir. What oftenest tempts you to disobey? As she did not immediately answer, he turned to the rest, and asked them all, what tempted them most, which led to some observations to each. At last he said to her, Do you often feel inclined to disobey your mother? Not often. Your father? No, never. Did you ever disobey your conscience with respect to your brothers and sisters? Yes, once. How long ago? About a year. Will you tell it? My brother was sick, and worried and troubled me, and I was impatient to him, and hurt his feelings. Shall you ever forget this? I don't know. Who else here have done as this little girl says she did? Most held up hands. Do you remember any particular instances? Several did, and one told that once, when his brother was sick, he was cross, and said to him, Before I would make believe being sick! Did you ever, said Mr. Alcott to the little girl, disobey your conscience with respect to people out of your own family? Yes, sometimes. And did they know it? Yes, I suppose they did. Do you think you love to obey your father and mother, and teachers, and conscience? Yes. And generally find yourself ready to do so? Yes. Do the rest of you? Some said, Yes; some said, No. How many wish you did love to obey more than you do? Many did. Have any of you failed to-day? Several. What do you call people that readily obey? They answered severally, good, obedient, kind, honest, obliging, generous, charitable, liberal, self-denying, good-natured.

Do you know what the word *docility*, *docile*, means? Tame, said one; I have heard it applied to animals. Mild and gentle, submissive, easily governed, were some other answers. Do you think this little girl is docile? All held up their hands. Do you think so yourself? After a pause she said, Generally. What does *docile* mean in the dictionary? They took their dictionaries, and found that Johnson said teachable. He told them to put them up. Some did not obey. Are you docile? said he. Instantly every book was put up.

CONSCIENCE.

To-day, Mr. Alcott remarked that the little girl generally questioned was not present; and he took out a little boy of five, and began with remarking, We have learned that spirit loves, trusts, is docile, or obedient; but there is much more to say about obedience. Little boy, he continued, we are going to find out, not whether you have good health, or have knowledge, or enjoy yourself, but whether you are good. What makes us good? Conscience. What is conscience? It is the spirit speaking. Have you any conscience? Yes. How do you know? My mother told me so. When? Why, once she was washing my face and hands, and I did not want to have her; and she told me that people would think my conscience was dirty, if my body was dirty; and so I asked her what my conscience was, and she said it was what told us right and wrong. Well, did you look within, and find there was conscience? Yes. Such of you as think you were told of conscience before you found it out, may hold up your hands. Most of them did. How many of you think your conscience began to be when you were told of it? Some did; and the little boy added, There was a spirit before. Was not this the way with you: there was a feeling before, and your mother made a thought of the feeling? Oh, yes! Some, however, thought there was a time when there was neither a feeling nor a thought. Can you conceive that the spirit lived before your bodies were made? Most of them said, Yes. About half-a-dozen, including the older ones, thought it was not possible.

Mr. Alcott then said, I observe that those who cannot conceive of spirit without body existing in God before it comes out upon the earth are the very ones who have required the most discipline and punishment, and have the least love of obedience. The rest are those who exercise most self-control, and seem to have the most conscience. Have you all conscience? Yes. How did you get it? No one knew. At last a boy of seven (mentioned once before) said, God gives us our consciences. When? Why, when we have learned right and wrong, God sends us conscience to make us do right. So I think, said the oldest boy in school. Is it born in the soul, said Mr. Alcott, or does God add it to the soul? He adds it. Is it something new? Yes. Do the rest think so? No one agreed. And the oldest boy said, It is in the soul, but it does not act till there is knowledge. Does it ever act, then, fully? No. True; there is much in the spirit that can never be represented in thought, or acted out, at least on earth. And so, little boy, when you went to be washed, you did not ask of conscience whether you were going to act right or wrong while you were being washed? No; I was a very little boy, and I used to think, if I did not do what was right, my mother would punish me. Was that all you thought about right and wrong, — being punished and not being punished? Yes, that was all. Well, what do you think about it now? Now I think of Pilgrim. What part of "Pilgrim's Progress"? Fighting Apollyon, said the child. Do you think you should be better if you never were punished? No; for I should wish to do wrong, and it would be wrong to wish to do wrong.

How many of you think your wishes are almost always good? Two boys held up their hands. How many think their wishes are too often bad? Two; and the little boy questioned was one. When you wish to do wrong, what stops you? My conscience; when I want to hug very little children so hard that it would hurt them, and I very often do, my conscience stops me. Does your conscience go into your mind and find out a reason for not hugging these little children? Yes; the reason is, it would hurt them to be hugged so hard. Did you ever wish to strike? No, never in my life. How far does your desire to hurt by hugging carry you? Why, as far as my conscience lets me go. This child speaks very slowly, which aids his meaning.

How many of you keep all your feelings within the limit which conscience says is right? Not a single one held up his hand. When conscience does limit your feelings within the bounds of right, what spiritual action do you perform? Obedience, said several. Mr. Alcott again turned to the little boy, and said, Supposing you should say, when you wanted to do some particular thing, Oh! I must do it (though conscience says, No); and so you do a little worse than conscience would allow to-day, and to-morrow you go a little farther, and to-morrow a little farther. What sort of a boy should you be at last? Just such a boy as —— (he named one of the worst boys in school). Can you do wrong, and escape punishment in your mind? No, never; it always makes me worse. Suppose a boy is angry, what is the punishment in his mind? Why, he feels as if he could take the world and break it into two pieces, tear it in halves; and, Mr. Alcott, will you let me tell you what part of "Pilgrim's Progress" I like best? Yes, said Mr. Alcott. It is where Mr. Greatheart is killing the Giant Despair. Is there any Mr. Greatheart in you? Yes, and he is just killing the Giant Despair; for once I thought I should never be good. Why not? Why, I would get tired sitting, and so leave off doing something, and look around. Should you like to be very good? Oh, yes! How good? Good as I can be. Who was the best man in the world? Lafayette. Was he the very best? Oh, no! it was Jesus Christ; I am surprised I could forget that. How many of you think, said Mr. Alcott, that you can be as good as Jesus

Christ in another world? Several held up their hands. Do any of you feel in despair, as if you never could be what you want to be? Several held up their hands. One said he was in despair of doing what he wanted to do with his mind. What do you want to do with it? He could not explain. Several said they wanted to be good. One said he would go through fire to be good. Another said he wanted to have a strong mind. Strong thoughts or feelings? Strong thoughts. Another wanted to be good, and to do good. Yes, said Mr. Alcott, part of being good is doing good. I cannot conceive of being good without the goodness shaping itself into actions. Several wanted to have self-knowledge. One wanted to have self-control. Another wanted to be generous. Such of you, said Mr. Alcott, as think you came into the world to do all these things you have spoken of, may hold up your hands. All held up their hands. Do you know recess-time is passed, half an hour? No, said all, with great surprise, looking at the clock. Well, there is still half an hour. You may take half of it for recess; or I will read from Krummacher. They decided to hear the reading, and he read

THE VOICE OF CONSCIENCE.

A rich man, named Chryses, gave orders that a poor widow and her five children should be driven out of one of his houses, because she was unable to pay the rent. But when his servants came to her, the woman said: Oh! grant a little delay; perhaps your master may take pity on us: I will go to him and implore his forbearance.

The widow thereupon went to the rich man with four of her children (for one of them lay sick), and they all earnestly entreated that they might not be turned out. But Chryses said, I cannot recall my commands; unless you pay forthwith what you owe me, you must go.

The mother then wept bitterly, and said: Alas! the attendance on my sick child has consumed all my earnings and prevented me from working. And the children prayed with their mother that they might not be cast out.

But Chryses turned from them, and went forth to the pavilion in his garden, and lay down according to custom on a couch to repose himself. It was a sultry day, and close to the pavilion flowed a stream which diffused refreshing coolness, and the air was so serene that scarcely a breeze stirred.

Then Chryses heard the murmur of the reeds on the banks, but it sounded to him like the moaning of the children of the poor widow; and he became uneasy upon his couch. He then listened to the noise of the stream, and it was as though he lay on the shore of a boundless sea, and he turned upon the pillow. When he again listened, the thunder of a rising tempest pealed at a distance, and then he felt as if he heard the trump of the last judgment.

He then rose forthwith, and hastened to the house, and commanded his people to admit the poor widow again into the cottage; but she had gone forth into the wilderness with her children, and was nowhere to be found. The storm meanwhile approached, and the thunder rolled, and the rain descended in torrents. And Chryses walked to and fro, and was full of uneasiness.

On the following day, Chryses received tidings that the sick child had died in the forest, and that the mother had gone away with the others. Then did the garden and his pavilion and his couch become hateful to him, and he no longer delighted in the coolness of the murmuring stream.

Chryses soon afterwards fell sick, and in the heat of the fever he incessantly heard the murmur of the reeds, and the noise of the stream, and the faint rolling of the approaching thunder. And so he gave up the ghost.

WILL.

Mr. Alcott began the next analysis, March 11th, by first asking questions to define the word *power*. Is power in you, or out of you? One said, Out of you; that is, out of your soul; but it is in the body. The rest simply agreed that power was in us: On being asked what one word included all the powers of the human being, one said, Will. Mr. Alcott asked if these powers were always in action. Yes, was the answer; which was afterwards modified, on their being led to see that we felt more and thought more at some times than others.

He then asked questions to define the word *quicken*.

It was decided that to quicken a thought or feeling was to call it forth into action. He asked such as thought that they had been quickened since they came to this school, to hold up their hands. Many did so. What has quickened you? They severally and simultaneously replied, *Your* spirit; *Your* conscience; Your *life*.

He then asked questions to define the word *tempt*. He described a temptation, without using the word, and they recognized it. What is the object of temptation? said he. To quicken the powers, was the final answer. He asked several of them what tempted them most? A little boy answered, I cannot tell yet, I have not done — (thinking, he meant). Many answered, Play; Pleasure; Appetites. Some did not know. The thinker at last said, he wanted to pull people about more than any other wrong thing. Who says they were never tempted? No one. He described a temptation, and a resistance to it, and asked what would be the effect upon their spirits of going through such exercises? They answered that they should grow stronger in spirit. Such of you as think you grow stronger in spirit, by resisting temptation, hold up your hands; do you understand how it is? They all thought they did. Such of you as think you have already weakened your spirits by yielding to temptation may hold up your hands. All the hands went up.

When he had asked many questions to define the word *discipline*, he said, Who have been disciplined in this school? Many. Who feel they have needed discipline? The same. Who think Mr. Alcott disciplines your minds? All. Who think that they are in a better state of discipline than they were? All.

Who has often said, I will? All. Who has had the feeling that leads to saying, I will not? All held up their hands. You all have a will? Yes. Do you expect to have your will brought out in this school? Yes. How? By its being tempted, said one. And disciplined, said Mr. Alcott; but where does will act? Within. In your body, soul, mind, all? Yes. How many think you have understood all that has been said pretty well? All.

He then asked questions to define the words *sense* and *flesh;* and then to define the word *obedience*, and then discriminated obedience to conscience, from obedience to flesh and sense. Can any one obey the conscience unless they have confidence in it? No. Who has no confidence in his conscience? None. If you do believe in your conscience, and have confidence in its teachings, what spiritual principle have you? Faith. How many mind me, because they would be punished if they did not? None would admit that they obeyed him from any other principle than faith in him. Some, however, confessed to particular instances of obeying him from fear of punishment.

What is that within you which sometimes carries you on as if you could not help it, and against your thoughts; urging you on, you do not know why and how? Some said, Soul. He then referred to birds building their nests; and several said, Instinct; but others seemed to think that human beings could not have instinct. Mr. Alcott then spoke of the motions, &c., of a very young infant; and some said they were instinctive. One boy said they were imitation. Another asked if imitation was not instinct. Mr. Alcott then spoke of the instincts of the various scholars, which accounted for their characteristic movements, &c., much to the amusement of all; and seemed also to define the word. He ended with asking if all understood instinct now. All said, Yes. Is it in the mind, or soul, or body? said Mr. Alcott; that is, is it in what thinks, or what feels, or in the body? It is in what feels, in the soul, said one. But it acts in the body, said another. Do you all think so? Yes.

How many of you know that you live? All. How did you find it out? They did not know. Does a little infant know it lives? Some said, Yes; some, No. Do you remember the time when you did not know you lived? No. How many think you felt before you knew it? How many think you knew it first? None. Does a little infant feel the air when it is fanned? Yes, and it wants to take hold of the fan, said one; It wants to eat the fan, said another. If a person could not feel the air, or pain, what would he be? One said, I should say he was *a thing*. Another said, He would be a body. Another said, I should say he had no soul. How many of you have heard the word *susceptible?* Many hands went up, and it was explained to the rest. What are you susceptible of? Pain; Pleasure; Love; Truth; were the various answers.

Do you know you are in this room? Yes. How many have heard the word *conscious?* Is it the mind or the soul which is susceptible? The soul. Is it the mind or the soul which is conscious? The mind. Consciousness is in the mind, said Mr. Alcott; and instinct is in the soul; is that it? Yes. Where is imagination? In the mind. Where is love? In the soul. Reason? In the mind. Knowledge? In the mind. Affection and passion? Instincts of the soul. Imagination, reason, and sense of things are the consciousness of the mind, said Mr. Alcott; and instinct, affection, and aspiration are the feelings of the soul? Yes.

At two different times, there was reading during the last winter, with especial reference to the subject of Temptation; one was the account of the temptation in Paradise Lost; and one was from Genesis; and when Mr. Alcott had finished reading, he asked all round, what new idea had been gained. Some said they had learned that they had gardens to superintend. Mr. Alcott asked what was the tree of temptation to them, and each answered, which involved a good deal of particular confession. One little boy said, he thought the tree of life was God; that God formed himself out into a tree. Did you ever see the tree of life? said Mr. Alcott. I suppose I did when I was born, said he; but I don't remember how it looked, for now I only see God with my mind. And what is the tree of temptation? Indolence and error, and anger and passion, said he. Perhaps the whole world is a temptation, said Mr. Alcott; every thing which you see? No, I do not think that; I think part of the world is the garden of God, and part of the world is the garden of naughtiness. God is on our right hand, and the garden of naughtiness is on our left. I asked him if the spirit might not be considered the garden of God, and the body the garden of naughtiness? He smiled, and said, Yes. And when you let your body govern you, you are in the garden of naughtiness; and when you let your mind govern you, you are in the garden of God? Yes, said he.

Mr. Alcott then questioned them on the scale. Look at this scale. You see the spirit, which manifests itself in search after Good, loves, trusts, obeys; and what is its law? Conscience, said they. Is not the spirit power? Yes. Suppose a being does not love and trust and obey Good according to conscience, has he any spirit? No. Has he no power? Yes. Suppose a person's action begins at the second division, what is the object? Pleasure; enjoyment. The object of the soul, then, is pleasure? Yes. And what is the law? They did not know. Is it not desire? Yes. Is enjoyment the same as goodness? Not always. Good is to be attained at the expense of enjoyment, sometimes? Yes. Is there any one word which includes the two meanings of enjoyment and good? After a while, one girl said, Happiness. Soul does not mean the same as spirit then? I thought it did, said one. When the soul loves, trusts, and obeys, then it is truly spiritual, or a pure spirit.

Where does spirit come from? From God. Yes, said Mr. Alcott, when the soul beholds God, it becomes spiritual. Spirit is life. Life comes from God. Spirit comes from God into the soul, and may be tempted to become appetite, affection, passion. What does *tempted* mean? It means tried. Can a good spirit be tried, tempted? There was no answer to this question; and he opened the Bible and read the temptation of Christ, paraphrasing the word *devil* as appetites, passions, false ideas, — in short, whatever feeling or thought may lead away from virtue. By the first temptation was shown the principle on which the appetites were to be resisted. Man does not live by bread alone. It is his body only that lives by bread; but there is something more than body in a man; something which lives upon what comes from God. "Every word" means every manifestation of God in things and beings. By the second temptation, he showed on what principle the passion of ambition, or of working by splendid self-displaying prodigies, was to be resisted. We should put our trust in general principles, and not in the expectation of extraordinary interpositions; for to trust in the power of goodness and truth shows the highest kind of faith. By the third temptation, he showed the principle on which the desire to use pious frauds, and the plans of a narrow expediency, are to be resisted; sincerity being the true worship of God. All this was brought out, not without a great deal of talk, in which I joined, and so lost the Record. In the beginning, one of the boys laughed as soon as Mr. Alcott said the word *devil* (having a ludicrous association with it). Mr. Alcott asked, What does devil mean? An evil spirit. An evil spirit within you, or out of you? Out of me. How many of the rest think the word *devil* represents a shape out of your mind? About half held up their hands. How many think the word *devil* represents all that tends to wrong-doing within you? All held up their hands but two, who persisted in saying that they thought the devil had a shape out of the mind.

As the little girl, who was generally questioned, on this day of analysis was not present, a boy of ten years of age took her place. Mr. Alcott began with asking, when a soul resisted temptation. When it does not give up to the body, said the boy. Is the law of the flesh the same as the law of the spirit? No. What is the law of the flesh? Desire. What is the law of the spirit? Conscience. If a boy gives up his conscience to his desire, he subjects the law of the spirit to the law of the flesh? Yes, he yields to temptation. Suppose you sit down to a table where there is every thing good to eat and drink (he went on and described a great many luxuries), what part of your nature is tempted? Appetites. How many of you seek to gratify your appetites? [He enlarged, and made graphic descriptions of common temptations to the appetites, which elicited a good deal of confession from all the boys.] He here read from Spenser the description of Gluttony, in the train of Lucifera.

Do you think, said he to the boy who was especially questioned, that you obey the law of the flesh, or the law of the spirit, with respect to your appetites? He said the law of the spirit. Always? Always. Do you never desire any gratification for your body, to a degree that wars against the law of the spirit? No. All the boys smiled at his self-complacency, which they seemed to think might proceed from self-ignorance. Mr. Alcott reminded him how impatient he was of cold last winter, much more impatient than many others. Some anecdotes were then told of fortitude and self-denial in children, by way of awakening in him a higher sense of spirituality than he seemed to have; for it was the want of an adequate sense of the law of the spirit, which made him feel that he obeyed it, when in truth he is a good deal controlled by the law of the flesh.

Mr. Alcott then asked all the school such questions as these: How many of you are apt to trouble your parents about your dress, because you cannot bear any little annoyance, or it does not gratify the appetite of the eye? How many give way to anger? How many can bear an insult? Not one boy thought he could bear an insult without revenging; and some said, that they ought not. Did Jesus Christ bear insults? Yes. Did he return them with injury? No. But if you are insulted, ought you to return it with injury, — so great a wrong is done you! They were silent. Is it the law of the spirit, or of the flesh, which makes you want to strike? Of the flesh. Which law is it that makes you want to speak harshly, when so spoken to? The law of the flesh. Did Jesus Christ revile when he was reviled? No. Did he strike when struck? No. Did he let his disciples fight for him? No. Why not? There was silence. What was there in his spirit that prevented it? Love, said a little girl. How many of you desire to obey the law of the spirit, instead of the law of the flesh, upon this subject? Many held up their hands, and the boy questioned among the number; but he said he could not help revenging an insult. You acknowledge your weakness on this point? Yes. — Mr. Alcott and I both agreed that this weakness, which he was willing to confess, was not so great in his case as the other weakness, which he would not confess. However, we said nothing. In one point he was true to himself: he was true to his own want of moral courage. No one who compared his answers, during this analysis, with those of the two former children, could fail to see the difference between their absolute simplicity and his non-committal spirit.

Well, some of you desire to obey the law of the spirit? what is the difference between desire and resolution? Resolution has will in it; Resolution has thought in it; Resolution has self-denial in it; Resolution is spirit, — were the various answers. How many of you have seen people in the world who can refrain from revenge? Many thought they had. How many respect yourselves the more, when you have given up to your passions? None. Do you know that revenge is the principle of murder: how many have felt this murderous principle? Several. How many think you have power within you, if you will use it, to master the desires of the body? Many did. Three boys thought they had not. How do you expect the power will come? said he to one. I do not expect it will come. What! God has sent you into the world, and told you to seek good, and yet you expect never to feel the power! Have you no spirit? He was silent. Oh, you have a giant spirit within you, stronger than all the earth: it will remove mountains if you will call upon it.

One of the boys here said, It is twelve o'clock. Who think it a punishment to be here? said Mr. Alcott. None. Who think it a reward to come to school? All. How many think there would be no punishment here, if the law of the spirit was obeyed? All. How many of you think that all my punishments are to bring you back to the law of the spirit? All. Why do you not come under the law of the spirit of yourselves? There was no answer. I kept a school once, in which there was no punishment; but the reward was, to come and see me twice a week in the evening, or to stop with me half an hour after school. How many would like it, if I had this reward now? Several held up their hands. Why? One said, I should like the instruction; another, I should be benefited; &c.

Well, said Mr. Alcott to the boy thus analyzed, you have been weighed in the balance to-day, and, even according to your own opinion, have been found wanting in one respect: perhaps you have felt yourself wanting on both points on which we have conversed.

APPETITES.

Mr. Alcott said, Shall any one want any thing, during our lesson? Seven or eight boys asked for water, and Mr. Alcott took the pitcher and a cup, and went to each and gratified the want. He remarked that this was a practical illustration of the subject of the day, — Appetites. One boy who had asked said he would wait till recess; but Mr. Alcott insisted on his drinking.

Having done this, he said, The soul wants to satisfy itself in its search after pleasure. This want is called Desire. Desire is the law of the soul. What is a law? A command, said one. Something that must be done, said another. Is there desire in appetite? Yes. What is appetite? It is a part of the soul, said a boy of five. Several said, No; appetite grows out of the body. Suppose the body dead, said Mr. Alcott, is there appetite in it? No. Why not? Because it is not alive. What made it alive? The soul. Then appetite is in the soul, and operates through the body; is not that it? There was still a doubt, and he went on, It is common to confound the organs of appetite with the appetites; but can you not conceive there could be appetite without a body? They could not conceive of this. Does the eye see? A boy of five said, When we look on any picture, there is a picture reflected into the inside of our eyes, and the mind sees it. But you know, said Mr. Alcott, there are some pictures which we see by our imagination. Well, said the child, the way that is I will tell you:

The pictures we look at, out of us, go into our minds, and change, and mix up, and come before our minds in new forms. Do these pictures come into our outward eyes? Oh, no! our mind looks into itself, and sees them. As many of you as think the soul sees by the eyes, and that the eyes would not see if it were not for soul, may hold up your hands. They all did. As many of you as think the appetites are the soul seeking for pleasure by organs, as the soul looks out by an organ of vision, hold up your hands. Only a part did; and one boy, who did not, said, People do not always have appetite, though they all have bodies. The sick have no appetite.

Mr. Alcott replied, Appetite is not merely after food, but for any bodily gratification or easement. He then asked if they thought the desire of sleep an appetite? the desire of motion? the desire of sweet sounds? the desire of seeing beauty? the desire of smelling sweet odors, and of touching delicate things? Most of them agreed that these seemed to them appetites. Well, said he, do not all these desires manifest themselves in the body? Yes. Yet they are soul? Yes. What do the appetites want? Food, said one. All outward things, said another. Are outward things adapted to the soul's appetites? Yes. Do you think there is enough in the world to satisfy the appetites? Yes. Is there enough outward to satisfy the soul's spiritual wants, its love, faith, power? None held up their hands.

How do you know when the appetites have obtained

enough? We are satisfied, said the little girl analyzed. What is the law? Satisfaction. Is not temperance a better word? said Mr. Alcott. And are you temperate in your desire for these gratifications we have mentioned? Generally. In what do you find yourself most liable to fail? She did not know. Have you an inordinate desire for food? No. Do you eat to gratify your taste, or to satisfy your hunger? For the last. Do you drink any thing to please your taste? No. Do you pursue amusement beyond the rule of temperance? Sometimes; but not without thinking of conscience, said she, adding the last part of the sentence as an after-thought. A boy here said there was no use in carrying conscience into play. She said she could not conceive how we could help carrying conscience into all we do. Mr. Alcott said, Every thing, even amusement, has a tendency to good or evil, and conscience always speaks on that question.

This gave rise to conversation on the subject of amusements, and the character of plays, and their effects on the habits of the mind and heart, and the duty of having plays that will cultivate and purify the imagination. Some anecdotes were told to illustrate the evil of playing with no plan, and of playing like brutes; and the good effects of playing beautiful imaginative plays. Mr. Alcott described a place of amusement, which should be fitted up with every embellishment that art could afford; and in which there should be every assistance that sympathy with youthful joyance could give. They were very much delighted; and he asked if such a place on Boston Common would not change the character of Boston boys? They thought it certainly would.

Then he said, What do you think you should be, if the restraining power of conscience was taken off? The various answers were: Bad; Just like Satan; A fool; A monkey; A donkey; A snake; A slave; A liar; An idiot; A toad. (I could not help telling Mr. Alcott afterwards that I was struck with the names of these animals; for every one seemed to hit upon the very animal he did resemble.) One girl said, I should do a great many bad things; another said, I should do all the wicked things that can be thought of; and a little boy said, I should not know any thing; I should be a kind of a drunken person.

Now as many as disobey conscience sometimes may hold up their hands. They all did. Well, you become, in the same degree as you disobey, just what you would become if you had no conscience. Who has done wrong to-day? Many held up their hands, and then confessed the particulars. What is the result of our analysis to-day? That this little girl is temperate in seeking gratifications of her appetites.

THE AFFECTIONS.

Mr. Alcott took the Bible to read from it. He then asked some questions to bring their minds into attention. One was, Do you know what the meaning of the word *affection* is? They all held up their hands. Then we are not going to speak of a subject of which you know nothing. How many think it is an interesting subject to talk about? Several. How many think it is interesting to feel affection? All. Who, of all persons that you have heard of, knew the most about affection? was it Jesus Christ? Yes. I am going to read this morning what he says about friendship.

He began: They were at supper, Jesus and his friends, it was their last supper together. He was going very soon to do something which would show what friendship was; but first he was going to talk about it. Shall you be interested to hear what he said? Many held up their hands. If there are any who wish rather to go into the anteroom than to hear this reading, they may go. There was considerable demur, when about eight concluded to go. He stopped them, and asked them if they thought it right to go. And having called up many reasons why they should not, by asking them questions, so that some concluded they would prefer to stay, the rest went. When they had been gone a little while, he went out and called them all in.

He then asked some more questions, and proceeded to read. The paraphrase of the conversation at the supper was very beautiful. He then laid aside the Bible, and arranged the school for the analysis.

Is conscience the law of affection? Yes. Could there be any love without conscience? Silence. Can you like another without conscience? Here was a difference of opinion. Do you like anybody whom you do not love? Yes. Do you love anybody whom you do not like? No. Do any of you think the body loves? No. Do the appetites love? They love good eating. Do you love to eat or like to eat? Some said they loved, and some said that they liked the object of appetite. Loving, said Mr. Alcott, is all it seems, and much more; liking seems more than it is. Who think it is wrong to like to eat, like to play, &c.? One said, It is sometimes right, and sometimes wrong. Liking is not wrong, said Mr. Alcott; but who think it is wrong to like these things better than our spirits? Most held up their hands. That is the very mistake that the drunkard, the sluggard, the glutton, and all who love their appetites, make. You have all of you been drunk, not with rum or wine, but with amusement, with pleasure. There was a good deal of answer to this remark, which was completely understood.

Who think it is wrong to have pleasure? Some held up their hands. Do you think so? I do not; but how are we going to find out when we have pleasure enough? By conscience, said one. Yes, the bowl is at our lips; but conscience says, That's enough; conscience takes care even of our bodies. He made some personal applications, and then went on: You know it is the spirit that sees, that feels, that touches, &c. Suppose God had so made our bodies that every time the spirit wanted to see, hear, taste, touch, smell, eat, drink, or move, it must be accompanied with some pain of the body; would life be as it is now? No, said they. No, continued he; God has accompanied all these things with pleasure; yet we abuse his goodness sometimes, and act for bodily pleasure itself. Is not that ungrateful and foolish? But the drunkard, because when he drinks it gives him pleasure, thinks that he will drink.

Does conscience rule over your pleasures? said he to the little girl analyzed. Yes. When you sit down to table with your father and mother, and brothers and sisters, do you carry conscience with you? Yes. Some people only carry their bodies to the table, and they talk all the time about what they are eating, and how good it tastes. He pursued the questions, Do you carry your conscience to play, to church, to bed, everywhere, and under all circumstances? (particularizing.) Yes. The others also answered, and thought they carried it, especially to church. I said, I know some children in the room who do not carry conscience to church. Mr. Alcott said, Conscience goes with you, at any rate; but I asked if you carried it, if you tried to be conscious of it? They seemed to doubt. How many of you ever think there is a right and a wrong way to play? Many did. Do you always carry conscience with you to play? On second thought, the little girl thought she did not. Probably none, said Mr. Alcott, always feel conscious of conscience; sometimes their likes, their appetites, or their flesh (as the Scripture calls it, because their appetites express themselves in the flesh), get the mastery over their spirits. But you said there was conscience in affection; what do you mean? Conscience makes us love good people. And keep faithful? said I. Yes.

Who think they love the spirit better than their

bodies? Many did. Who prove it by their actions? Several held up their hands. Who would like to have me see all that they do; and think it would prove to me that they love spirit better than they like their bodies? One girl thought it would make no difference. One boy doubted. Most thought they should not like it.

Well, this little girl, said Mr. Alcott, thinks she has found something better than eating or drinking, or seeing or tasting, or touching or smelling; that she has got out of her appetites and senses. He then imagined a fowler and his net, which illustrated the temptation of the senses; and asked if any of them were ever caught in this net. They all confessed. Who spread this net? No answer. Which one of you, when you see a person who does not look just as you would like, who does not gratify your eyes, finds it hard to like him? Some held up their hands. Those who held up their hands, Mr. Alcott said, were caught in the net of sense. He supposed the case of a boy offered to the school, described as full of excellence, as a beautiful boy, thinking of his mind, and the next day he should come, and his face should be plain, not so beautiful as was expected; how would it be? Some said that spiritual and material beauty were never disjoined. There was recess.

ASPIRATION.

We are going to talk to-day about the desire of growing better; of aiming high, and at a great deal: what word expresses this kind of action? They severally said, Sensibility; Faith; Love; Virtue; Spirituality; Aspiration.

Aspiration, said Mr. Alcott, what does that mean? To go up. What goes up? The spirit. For what? For goodness and truth. Who knows a person that aspires? Nearly all held up their hands. Are they now living in a body? Almost all put down their hands. Name those alive. Dr. Channing and Mr. Taylor were named. Whom did the rest mean? Jesus Christ. Mr. Alcott said, Yes; and Jesus said, If any one aspires to follow me, he must give up his appetites and false affections, and go earnestly to work to do difficult things. How many of you aspire in that way? Several thought they did.

Who says that we should aspire after what we can see with our eyes? One boy said he did not see why we should not. Who says we should not? Several. Why, what were eyes made for? To see with, said one. To help our spirits, said another. How can they help our spirits? The eyes can see the works of God, which show our spirits his wisdom, and they can read the Bible. When we look at any thing, do we see it all? We do not see the happiness it gives, but we feel it, said one. Some others thought we saw the whole of what we looked at. Mr. Alcott called on a boy to rise and stand in the middle of the room. Do you see that boy? I see his body, said one. Is there any thing which you do not see, that helps to make up the thought of that boy? Yes, his feelings; his thoughts; his spirit; said they severally. What is the use of seeing his body? It is the sign of his spirit. Shut your eyes and imagine him; can you? Yes. Who sees this piece of crayon? Many. Professor Silliman would convince you that you saw but little of it. One boy said, I have seen my own spirit many a time. You are thinking of insight. Who now think they should aspire after what we can see with our eyes? One boy. Who think we should never seek after outward things, except as signs of something better, more spiritual? All, without exception. I know persons, said Mr. Alcott, who look after outward things always, and for present pleasure, without thinking whether they are signs. One boy here has said to me that he could not like a person who was not handsome. I did not say I could not, but that I did not, said the boy; and I cannot help it.

Who think there is a beauty more beautiful than any thing their eyes see? Several. Who think the action of the good Samaritan was a beautiful action? All. Is love beautiful? Yes. Who have done a beautiful action? (He explained by instancing beautiful purposes, and their enaction.) A few held up their hands. Are you willing to tell what they were? No one was. You think perhaps it would take away its beauty to tell it? All again held up their hands.

Now all tell me, which you think you ought to do,—aspire after beautiful thoughts, beautiful feelings, beautiful actions, or beautiful outward things? All said the former; but the æsthetic added, Beautiful things too. Oh, yes! said Mr. Alcott, or we should have to throw away all our pictures and busts. Portrait and all, said the boys. Do you think I value that portrait for the form of the face, as it presents itself to the eye? No: you like him; you think he is good; you like his spirit, and so you think he is handsome, — were the several answers. Yes: the expression of his spirit seems to bring beauty to my eye, said Mr. Alcott. Now look at that bust of Socrates. A lady who came in here once, said: What an ugly thing that is! I want to put it under ground! Put Socrates under ground! exclaimed the children, with surprise. Yes, so she said; but I think of the mind of Socrates, his thoughts about beauty, his beautiful life, his beautiful death. Did you not think his death was beautiful when he drank the hemlock? Yes. Perhaps there is not a bust in the world that brings to mind so many thoughts of beauty as that does; for Socrates led people to think about beauty in itself. He was the teacher of Plato, the very philosopher of beauty. Here Mr. Alcott went towards the bust and touched the capacious cup of brain. What a brow this is! They all looked very reverent. He then went towards another cast, and said to a little boy, What does this represent? A child praying. Prayer is aspiration, said Mr. Alcott; the aspiration of the whole being towards its Father.

Now who think they have been misled by their eyes; have not looked deeper than the shape of things; have not thought enough of what things are the sign of? Many confessed. Well, it is a common fault. The Scripture calls this fault the lust of the eye. Mr.

Alcott said he had, in his youth, fallen into this snare. He had had an inordinate pleasure in pretty things, even in dress. He asked what mistake a dandy made. To think too much of personal appearance. How many think so much of dress as to trouble their fathers and mothers about it? Several held up their hands. Who are not at all particular? Several. Some of you perhaps make the opposite mistake, and are hardly tidy.

He then turned to the little girl who is generally analyzed, and said, Do you remember being deceived by your eyes? She had been, she thought; but could remember no instances.

Such of you as aspire after spiritual beauty, hold up your hands. All did. Such as aspire after material beauty? The æsthetic held up his hand again, and said, I want both. When God made the world, did he make things beautiful to deceive us; or to show us his own beauty, so that outward things might lead us to him? For the last. What did I say? You said God made the world beautiful, so that we might know he was kind and beautiful, said one. Can you understand, then, that the Beautiful may lead us to the True? Most held up their hands. And that the Beautiful and True are the sign of the Good? Yes. Then when you see any thing beautiful, you should find to what true thing it leads, and then find of what good thing it is the sign, and then you are very near God: what did I say, little boy? You said, said he, that Beauty is the sign of Truth, and Truth is the sign of Love, and God is Love. (This boy is five years old: the choice expression will be observed. Both Mr. Alcott's words and his have been carefully retained.) Do you want good, beautiful feelings? continued Mr. Alcott to him. Yes. When did you get some? To-day. When? As soon as you began to talk about the eyes.

Where did the beautiful thoughts you had this morning come from? said I to this child, at recess. Part came from the conversation, and some from God. (This idea, constantly expressed by this child, that his original thoughts come from God, is his own. At least, it was not gained at school; unless indirectly. No such expression has ever been used here.)

Such of you as know any person who, instead of aspiring, seems to go down, may hold up their hands. Many did. If you think any of your companions here aspire above your mark, signify it. Almost all did. Do you know of one here who seems never to have gone low? All did. Who is it? said Mr. Alcott to the little child of five. He named a boy of eight, in whose thoughts he always expresses interest. The rest of the boys smiled, and wanted to tell of whom they thought; but Mr. Alcott would not allow them to do so.

When they came in after recess, Mr. Alcott asked who had gained new ideas from the morning's conversation. Most held up their hands. What different classes of goods are there? He answered himself: Things, — outward goods; knowledge, — intellectual goods; and spiritual goods, — Faith, Hope, Charity, &c. Is knowledge a good, when it is used for our own rather than others' sake, and we are proud of it? They severally said, We should use it for others; For ourselves; For ourselves, but some also for other people. Is it aspiration to seek knowledge for our own good alone? No. Does a lawyer, who is using his knowledge to make himself admired and powerful, aspire? No. Does a school-teacher, who teaches in order to get money, aspire, even though he does help his scholars? No. Does it seem to you that the people you see are trying after spiritual good, generally? No. After intellectual good? Some of them. Do many people seem to be striving after money, houses, carriages, reputation? Yes. Do many seem to try to get money to do good with? A few. Who think people seem to be striving for money for themselves only? Several; and Mr. Alcott said, When did you find that out? To-day, said a boy of ten. When I was five years old, said a reflective and conscientious boy of eight.

A gentleman present here asked a series of questions, calculated to bring out their opinion of Mr. Alcott's disinterestedness; and they signified their undoubting confidence in it, not only by holding up their hands, but by jumping into their chairs, and stretching out both hands. So you think, was his last question, that some people aspire after something higher than physical good? Yes. Such of you as think Mr. Alcott would make as good use of his mind, as he does now, if he kept his thoughts to himself, signify it. They jumped down from their chairs, and said, No. The gentleman remarked to me, Mr. Alcott has his reward.

Where do you think Truth and Beauty are? resumed Mr. Alcott. In God. And there is some in our souls, said a little boy of five, after a pause. How do we get it in our souls? We ask God for it, and he puts it in. If we do not want it much, does he put it in? Oh, no! we must want it very much. Did you ever hear these words? said Mr. Alcott: Ask, and ye shall receive; seek, and ye shall find; knock, and it shall be opened unto you. Yes: Jesus Christ said them.

Who think that spiritual good is the best? All. Who think that, in aspiring after spiritual, we get all other good? All. Who said, Seek first the kingdom of heaven, spiritual good; and its righteousness, or act accordingly; and all these things shall be added unto you, for then they can do you no harm? Jesus Christ, said all.

Little girl, after all that has been said about aspiring, do you think you aspire after spiritual good more than any other? I think I do, said she. And next to that for the intellectual good which helps the soul, as the hand helps the body? Yes.

Who among you think that a school which does not aim at spiritual good has the right aim? None. Who have received some new thoughts to-day, which they think they shall remember always? Many. Who know themselves so well that they fear they shall forget? Several.

Who now think that they shall aspire to be the strongest and most cunning in their plays? None. Do you know what ambition is? Striving to get more than you have, said one. What is your ambition? I don't know. To be admired? No; but to have the best things. Who else says so? A younger one said, The best spiritual things; and many joined with him. Who has not much ambition? Several. Who will let things go on in their own way? One (who is very indolent). Who feel within power or will to do every thing? Almost all.

When they were dismissed, the visitor called a little boy of five to him, and said, Do you know what Jesus Christ meant by these words, "If you had faith, like a grain of mustard-seed, you could say to this mountain," &c. I have read it, said the child; but I do not remember what it represents. What does the mountain mean? said I. It is a mountain in the mind, said he, without hesitation. And the mustard-seed? A little faith, that will grow larger; and he bounded away to go home with his companions.

IMAGINATION.

Mr. Alcott began thus: Who enjoy this exercise? Several. Who have brought fresh minds this morning, ready to attend? Many. Who have dull minds this morning? None. One boy said his mind was fresh from the well! Fresh from what well? The well of the spirit, said he. Mr. Alcott went on: We are on Imagination to-day, the power of shaping thoughts: who think they shall be highly interested in this? All held up their hands but one boy, who was out of temper.

To the question, What do you mean by imagination? there were several answers, among which were the following: The power of conceiving thoughts in your mind, so as to see them with your eyes; The power that brings ideas out of your mind, so that others may see them; Thoughts that come out of your mind; To see things in your mind; To picture forth ideas; To see thoughts and feelings; To picture forth ideas and feelings in words, which have not come out in things; To picture out things in your mind a great deal more beautiful than any in the outward world. The last was the answer of the boy who at first was out of temper. He was interested in spite of himself.

Mr. Alcott here read the Transfiguration; and then asked, What does *transfigure* mean? To change the shape. What does *imagination* mean? To make new shapes. Did you ever feel any thing like this? did any of you ever see shapes, beautiful shapes, going out of your own minds? Many said, Yes. Two boys gave accounts of what they called visions. One said he often imagined Jesus Christ standing before his eyes. The other described a particular instance very minutely, of an angel coming with music, and the music seeming to be shaped. What is that faculty which is not imagination, but something like it? Fancy. Here he read the description of Queen Mab, as an instance of fancy; and then opened Coleridge's "Ancient Mariner," and read Parts III. and IV.

Which has the most shaping power in it, said he: this last, or the description of Queen Mab? The last, was the acclamation. Such of you as think you have fancy, and not imagination, hold up your hands. Several did. Such as have the most imagination. Several.

Such of you as think you have the power of putting all you think and feel into words, hold up your hands. Several did. Who say that they never yet found words that would hold all their thoughts and feelings? Several. Can you understand this definition? — Imagination is the power that represents, re-presents? Yes. Imagination represents spirit, soul, mind, the outward world, and God, said Mr. Alcott. Imagination is the power by which you picture out thoughts that never were realized in the world, as in "Pilgrim's Progress," said a child under six. Several more repeated the idea which Mr. Alcott had expressed, more or less exactly; none of them so fully as this boy had done. Do you know any one who has no imagination? Some said, No, except an idiot. Mr. Alcott said there were many people with uncultivated imaginations who were not idiots. Mr. Alcott asked the little boy who described the Angel of Day and Night, where he thought he got his imagination. He said he did not know he had imagination: he knew he had fancy. Mr. Alcott then asked the rest if they thought he had imagination. They all said, Yes: imagination and fancy too. Mr. Alcott then asked concerning each scholar; and they discriminated very well in regard to the individuals, showing that they had observed the operations of one another's faculties.

Mr. Alcott here described imagination as the life and

power of the spirit, the eagle that carries us up to high views; and said that it was the name of the mind in the highest action. He then asked, When imagination looks back, what is it called? Memory, said one. When it looks forward to the future, what is it called? One said, Curiosity; another, Expectation. Curiosity and expectation are in it, said Mr. Alcott. Foresight, said one of the girls. A boy of excellent understanding and little imagination said, Understanding. Mr. Alcott said, Oh, no! understanding sees only what is immediately around it.

JUDGMENT.

When the children were arranged for analysis, the most lawless boy in school was made superintendent, an employment which keeps him from wrong-doing. Mr. Alcott began: This hour is a pleasant one to those who look for realities within as well as without themselves; and he asked some questions to bring their minds steady. We are going to talk about judgment to-day. What is judgment? what do you do when you judge? do you guess? No, said one. A little boy of five, a new scholar, said, To judge is to know certainly. A boy of nine said, Judgment is to discriminate between good and bad, and see what to do. Do we judge only about actions? said Mr. Alcott. No: about feelings and quality and size. A boy of eight said, To judge is to think whether things are right or wrong. Another of the same age said, Judgment is examination. The power of judging, said Mr. Alcott, is one of the noblest which is given to man: where does it show itself in our nature? In the mind, said a boy of ten. In which faculty of the mind? In the understanding, said one; In the will, said another. It requires a great deal of thought to judge, said a boy of eight. What do you think of that boy who last spoke? said Mr. Alcott to the rest of the school. He is a good boy. How do you know? By his actions. How? This led to an analysis of the judgment in this one instance. He then named several buildings, and asked which was the most beautiful. They told their opinions, and he analyzed the process in this instance again. Can we get along in this world with judgment without comparing? No answer. What should you think of this: that a mind should see all things and subjects so quickly that it would know immediately how things were, and not feel that it was comparing or reasoning? It would be the judgment of an angel, said a boy of five, the new scholar. This room we can all look upon, and form a great many judgments upon at a glance. Suppose a little fly, having all the mind that we have, were to undertake to form these judgments: how much time it would take, and what a quantity of geometrical and other reasoning it would have to go through! The universe is a much wider space to us than this room would be to a fly. But this is about outward things. Which do you think is easier to judge of, outward things or ourselves? There was a difference of opinion; but the most reflective ones said, It would be easier to judge of ourselves, of inward things; for we could know what we were feeling and thinking better than what is around us and out of our sight; and we could know all about our own actions better than we could all about the actions of others.

Do we judge about every thing we do? We ought to do so, said one. When we look at the sun, and it dazzles us, ought we to judge whether it is best to shut our eyelid or not? said Mr. Alcott. Oh, no! it shuts of itself, said several. Then some of our actions are not the result of judgment, and cannot be made dependent upon judgment; but are what? They come by instinct. Can we make our judgments instincts; that is, as quick as instinct? Sometimes, said one boy, we do things which we might judge about, and which are wrong; but we do them by instinct: now how can we help that? what is that? It is passion; and passion is not judgment, is it? said Mr. Alcott. No. What is it? Instinct. Is instinct wrong? When it is mistaken for impulse, said Mr. Alcott; when it is not governed; when instinct is passion, it is wrong. How can we govern instinct so that it may not be passion? By reason and conscience, said several. Is there reason in judgment? Yes. Is there conscience in judgment? Yes. Is there will in judgment? Yes. Is the will which is in the judgment of conscience your own? It is my own, and God's also. What do you do when you judge? We think of a great many things. Do you compare? Yes.

In comparison and reasoning, do you go into yourselves? Yes. In comparing the things in the universe, and reasoning geometrically, &c., as we supposed the fly to do, should we go inward? Yes. Thus you see that, even in studying outward things, you are aided by something within? Yes. That which is within us must contain the idea of the outward world. And, to govern the spirit within us, and, by making it strong and loving, to put it in harmony with the Author, will enable the outward world to wake up within us its own image, and a sense of the beauty, power, goodness, and ideas of the Creator that produced it. (This perhaps was said in simpler language.)

But what is a standard, a rule of judgment, respecting inward things? No answer. There was One, whose very instinct was reason and conscience, and he is a standard; who was that One? An angel, said our new scholar. Jesus Christ, said another.

Well, said Mr. Alcott, let us hear what Jesus Christ says about judging and judgments. He read in paraphrase: Judge not without a great deal of care; for by the same standard as you judge others, you will be judged yourself. You show your own character by your judgments: if they are just and liberal and generous, it is because you have the sentiments of justice, liberality, and generosity within your own heart; for these are necessary in order to sympathize with the magnanimous sentiments of others.

You came to this school some months ago, with some notion in your heads about Mr. Alcott. You came day after day, and saw him do things, and heard him say words. Were you able to form a judgment of him immediately; or have you found that your opinions have altered? They have altered. How many of you have misjudged me? Many. How many of you have misjudged your companions, father, mother, brothers, sisters? Many; and one mentioned a particular instance. What is most necessary for us, that we may judge others correctly? To know ourselves. And we can judge of ourselves, of inward things, more easily than we can of outward things? Yes. Does the mind shape itself in the outward world, or does the outward world shape itself in the mind? It is God's mind that shapes itself in the outward world. And what is our mind? It is the image of God's. The human spirit is the image of the Divine Spirit? Yes. And is the human spirit's action an image of the Divine Spirit's action? Yes, sometimes; it ought to be. Can the human spirit shape itself, then, as the Divine Spirit does, in the outward world? Yes, by words. Only by words? Yes, by good actions. Only by words and actions? By paintings and sculpture. Good actions, poetry, painting, and sculpture are men's creations then? Yes. Do the good man, the poet, the painter and sculptor, think most of the inward or outward world? The inward. And they go from the inward to the outward world? Yes. And always find something or make something correspondent with the inward? Yes. They find the inward explains the uses, &c., of the outward? Yes. Then for judging of the outward world, as well as our fellow-beings, we must begin with ourselves? Yes.

INSIGHT.

Mr. Alcott took the Bible, and said: There are two laws which govern all things: one is the law of necessity, or force; the other is the law of — what? Love; good-will; conscience; the spirit, — were the several answers. Can any one who is governed by force have his liberty? No. What is the law of liberty? Love. The people of this country are free, said one boy; but it is not governed by love. I am not talking of political government, said Mr. Alcott. When we love good, and are left to do what we please, do we do right or wrong? We do right, said a boy of five, if we love right. Who acted very wrong yesterday afternoon, said Mr. Alcott, when I was unwell, and did not come to the school-room? Many stood up. You are not moral; your goodness depends on another; you are weathercocks; you have no principle; neither love, which is the law of liberty, nor conscience, governs you: is all that true? Most thought it was. Are you trustworthy? No. So your goodness depends on the presence of Mr. Alcott? Yes. Who think the law of force should be brought to bear on you? Many did. You know a thief is shut up because he abuses liberty? Yes.

Mr. Alcott then told the youngest boy in the class to go and touch the heads of all who, as he thought, would do right, if all punishment, all outward laws, &c., could be done away. He went and touched five heads, with excellent judgment. Mr. Alcott said, I believe all the best heads have been touched but one. He looked puzzled, and went to several who were next best. Mr. Alcott said, No, and it is no matter. He went to his seat. All the boys smiled at his unconsciousness, and one said, That is real.

Mr. Alcott then said, To-day, we talk of Insight. What is insight? Insight is looking into ourselves, said one. By what power do we look into ourselves? said Mr. Alcott. By insight, said another. Insight, said Mr. Alcott, is the spirit seeing itself; and seeing the outward world in spirit. Which of you have gone inward and viewed yourselves; seen with the spirit, and into spirit? None held up hands.

Who among you ever dream? All held up their hands. Are your eyes closed when you dream? Yes. Do your ears hear any sounds? No. Who has shed tears in sleep? Some. How did you hear, what did you see, when you saw and heard nothing outward, and yet shed tears in your dreams? Things seemed to happen, said one. Where do you think your mind was, when your eyes and ears were closed, and yet you saw and heard, and laughed and cried? A little boy said, My spirit was in God; my heart and soul and mind were in me, and—(he hesitated and said, Oh, Mr. Alcott!) Very well, said Mr. Alcott, smiling; that's enough. Who can answer that question? One said, Our minds left us; and God was within us. Is he more within us when we are asleep than when we are awake? said Mr. Alcott. Sometimes. After some more talk, the boy illustrated, thus: I have had the nightmare, and wanted to kill somebody, but thought it was wrong, though I was asleep.

Mr. Alcott spoke of the bad dreams of a glutton and intemperate man, and asked the children if they ever had bad dreams. He said that some people had bad dreams because they had sick bodies; sometimes these sick bodies were their own fault; sometimes they were inherited from faulty ancestors. (Some boys were sent out.) One boy's idea about dreaming was, that bad dreams came partly from bad minds, and partly from not having well bodies; generally the last. Mr. Alcott said that illness of body was to be ascribed to wrong-doing somewhere; and sometimes it was ignorant wrong-doing of our own or our ancestors. A good deal of talk arose, and some anecdotes were told.

Mr Alcott here read a dream from the Bible: it was the beautiful one in Job. He then read the dream of Jacob; and, after some conversation on its meaning, he said, Such of you as think you have an outlooking power, may hold up your hands. Several held up their hands. Who say they have not such a power? Several. Why, don't you see me? Yes. Who think they have such a power? All. Who think the power that looks out is deeper than the eyes? Several. Who think it is no deeper than the eyes; that only the eye looks? Several. We speak then of a power, an inward power that looks out of the eye: what is it called? Some said, Sight; some said, The mind; some said, The understanding; some said, The spirit. Mr. Alcott said, The soul has two great faculties, Insight and Outsight.

Some boys in this school have insight, and some outsight; and it would be very easy to show who have insight, and who have outsight, in the greatest degree, by thinking on what subjects each answers most readily. But all have both classes of thoughts, in a degree, said he: the power of seeing shapes without, and seeing the feelings and ideas in their own souls also.

I am going to read what St. Paul says about these two classes of thought, said he. And he read in paraphrase the last part of the fourth chapter of 2d Corinthians, and the first part of the fifth chapter.

He then addressed the little girl analyzed, by name. What is there in the outward world that you like best, that you think most beautiful? After a while she said, Nature. What objects in particular? No answer. Do you like flowers? Yes. Do you like running brooks? Yes. Do you like the ocean? Yes. Do you like the pebbles on the shore? Yes. Can you describe the feelings that you have when you see the ocean; imagine yourself there, how should you feel? The power, said she.

A series of questions were now asked as to the comparative effect of different scenes on the feelings of the several children; and some preferred ocean; some, mountains; some, rivers; some, caverns in the earth; some, cataracts; some, shells; some, stars, &c. He went on to ask questions which might show into what departments of natural history their tastes would lead them. He found some zoölogists, some geologists, some botanists, some astronomers, &c. One at last remarked that he liked machines, engines, &c. Many other boys agreed with him. Mr. Alcott said things were interesting to us, just in proportion as they seemed to be alive, or manifested spirit.

The next series of questions was calculated to bring out what was their taste for the Arts; and there was considerable variety of taste. Some were architects; some, painters; some, sculptors.

Who think dollars and eagles are very beautiful, and take great delight in seeing them? One boy said he took great delight in having them.

Who like carriages and splendid equipage? One said, I like sleighs. Another said, I like to be inside of them. Who like beautiful clothes, dresses? None. Those may stand up who would not play with beggar boys, even if they were good, because of their looks. Several rose, and Mr. Alcott said that many of those who were standing up would make the beggar boys worse probably; so it was very well. Who would play with beggar boys if they were good? Several rose with great emphasis. Who would not play with colored boys if they were ever so good and well instructed? The same boys rose as did at first. I am afraid your minds are colored with prejudices, said Mr. Alcott; and that you would darken their minds with your faults; so it is very well. The rest laughed, and, when those sat down, rose up and said they would play with black boys, if they had cultivated minds.

What if you were blind, and could not look out upon things at all; would there be any thing left to make you happy? He said this to the little girl analyzed. Yes, inward things, said the little girl. What inward things? Thoughts, feelings, a good conscience, &c., were named. Who are most truly blind, those who cannot see inward things, or those who cannot see outward things? Those who cannot see inward things. You know when we talked awhile ago, we said something about a net. Outward things, perhaps, form a net which catches our minds sometimes. Perhaps some of you are caught. I should like to see one person caught, said a little boy. Should you, said Mr. Alcott, like to see a boy whose eyes and ears are so caught by outward things that his mind is all taken up and never looks inward? Yes. Well, there he is, said Mr. Alcott, holding a looking-glass before him.

He then turned again to the little girl. Which power had you better use, the power of outsight or of insight? Insight. Why? Because it sees the real things. What are those things which the outsight sees? Shadows of real things. Now each one think, said Mr. Alcott, what idea have you gained from this conversation? One said, Insight is better than outsight. Another said, Inward things are better than outward things. Is that an idea in your head, or a feeling in your heart. I don't know, said she.

Suppose you saw a man born into this beautiful world, and all his life long he was running round to catch bubbles, every one of which broke in his hand. They all laughed. Or a man running after his shadow; and he went on with several similar analogies which made them laugh. Such are the persons, he said, who live for outward things instead of inward things.

Who say play is a bubble? Some held up their hands. But play is a very proper exercise in its place. Who say pleasure is a bubble? All held up their hands. Yet it is a bubble that it is innocent to look at a little. Is love a bubble? No. Is happiness? No. Is the soul? No. Is heaven? No. Is immortality? No. Who say they have no doubt about inward things, but about outward things there is an uncertainty? Several did.

Mr. Alcott then said, We will close with some words of Jesus, — words which he uttered when he lived in a body like ours: Lay not up for yourselves treasures on earth, where moth and rust do corrupt, and thieves break through and steal; but lay up for yourselves treasures in heaven (in the inward world), where moth and rust do not corrupt, nor thieves break through and steal.

GENERAL SURVEY OF THE ANALYSIS.

Mr. Alcott called the class to analysis, for the last time. He said we had now gone through the scale, but it had often been changed since we began, for almost every week had improved it. He then drew their attention to the one which was now on the blackboard, and said that the arrangement only was altered; for the same subjects were brought up by both scales.

We began with love, and then went to faith; and

then to conscience, speaking of obedience, temptation, and will; and then to the appetites, affections, and aspirations of the soul; and then we went to the mind, and spoke of imagination, judgment, and insight. To-day I intend to talk a little more about insight; and I shall read what Jesus Christ says about it. He says we should not strive to get outward things which may be stolen and corrupted; but we should strive to get things within, which cannot be taken away, because they are God's; for what we love will take up all our exertions.

He here stopped, and said that one of the boys in this school had said that he did not know, before he came to this school, that he had inward eyes; but now he felt that they were open. They began to guess who it was, but they did not guess the right one. Mr. Alcott said that some of them, when they came, were blind, were in midnight. And then he went on reading different passages of the Gospels. He ended with, The light of the body is the eye; what eye? This eye, said a little boy of five. That is the body's eye: what is the spirit's eye? That eye which can see every thing that it wants to see, and which can see God; the body's eye cannot see what it wants to, but the spirit's eye can; and, Mr. Alcott, I think that when we are asleep the spirit goes out of the body, and leaves the body dead; and by and by it goes back again, and makes the body alive again. But is the body entirely dead in sleep? said Mr. Alcott. Why, perhaps a little spirit stays in the body to keep it alive. But almost all the spirit goes out, and sees and hears with its inward eyes and ears; and that is dreaming.

Now let us take a survey of the whole, said Mr. Alcott. Such of you as think that the spirit acts in instinct may hold up their hands. No answer. As soon as a baby is born it cries; it seems to be astonished to find itself in the world, amidst so many things it does not know, and which are so unlike itself; not one thing it sees, or one word that it hears, does it understand; it cries — By instinct, interrupted one of the children. Yes, said Mr. Alcott; and it moves its hand to take hold of the sun or fire, or whatever it sees; for it does not know how far off things are, or what will hurt, and what will not. Is there not instinct in a baby's first motions? Yes. Does spirit act in instinct? Yes. Does spirit act in a baby when it loves its mother? Yes, a good deal, said one. Does spirit act in appetite? Yes. Does spirit act when it sees and wants something beautiful? Yes. What is that action? Aspiring. Does spirit act in thought? Yes; for the body cannot think. Thought, said Mr. Alcott, is the ladder by which spirit climbs up to heaven; i.e., into itself. Instinct, love, and faith go out from the soul. Thought goes back to the soul. By insight we go into the soul and see what is in ourselves. By judgment we compare thoughts. How many have insight? But a few thought they had. One of the most thoughtful said, A very little. Who do not go in for whole days? Two boys, one a lazy boy of eight, another a new scholar of five, held up their hands. Who cannot live a week without being taken captive and carried into the inward or spiritual world? No answer.

Who, every night before they go to sleep, go inward and think of what is within? Many. Who think of this over again in the morning? Several. You know that Jesus said, there was a fountain in there of living water, which springs up into everlasting life. What is this fountain? The spirit.

We talked about dreaming a good while ago: who among you dream? Several. Most of you dream when you are awake: you see things vaguely and dimly, not as if they all belonged together, but as if they were in disjointed pieces.

How many of you think God can be discovered with the eyes? None. Such as think you can see his works only with your body's eyes, and that he himself is to be found by looking within, with inward eyes, hold up your hands. All did. How many of you look within enough to know a good deal about God? None. How many do not? All. How many think it is hard? One indolent boy held up his hand. How many think an idle person can see God? Some. It was here found that some confounded idleness with repose; when all comprehended it, they all said no idle person could see God; and made the same answer to the questions, How many think an intemperate person can see God? An obstinate-willed person? An angry, passionate person? A person living for the outward? A liar, deceiver? There was some talk about the difference of liking truth in others, because it is convenient to ourselves, and loving it so as to speak and act it. Who think that those who love truth will probably know most of God? All. Who think that those who deny themselves, who try to control their feelings, even their love, will know most of God? All. Such as think those love God most who are willing to die and lose their body may hold up their hands. All did. Such as think that, to find God, we must keep all our nature in its right place; that no part should be asleep; that we should be like the child aspiring (he pointed to the cast), may hold up their hands. All. He then went on, making remarks on each of the scholars, and saying what parts of the nature of each he thought were asleep. This took a good while; but it was not lost, as it brought the subject home.

He then spoke of the effect of the passions: how, in the drunkard, appetite swallows up the nature; how, in the avaricious, the love of riches swallows up the nature; but when the spirit swallows up the nature, nothing is destroyed, but every part is strengthened and purified, and put in the right place.

Who think that we must know ourselves, in order to know God? All. Who thinks he cannot know God, till he knows himself a great deal? All. Who think that they can know God by studying outward things? None. What are outward things? Shadows of inward things, said the little girl, who was generally the subject of analysis. The representation of mind, said a boy of nine. Who was called the image of God?

Jesus Christ, said the whole school. Yes: the outward world is the image of the perfect mind; and Jesus Christ was the image of God; or his nature was all spirit, as he said. Who think that until we study ourselves, we cannot study outward things to much advantage? Many.

Mr. Alcott then remarked that some naturalists who never studied themselves, but studied outward things, did not believe in spirit; and some who believed in spirit, did not think it was the most important. Others have gone out into the outward world, thinking it a shadow of the inward, and followed on until they found the spirit that was in themselves, and God. One boy said, If I study botany, can I go on from it and find God? Mr. Alcott explained, but I could not hear him, as he walked to a place, where he stood with his back to me. Some remarks were made on the Free Inquirers, calculated to produce charitable feelings towards the honest among them.

What have these analysis lessons taught you? To know ourselves. Yes: your inward selves, your spirit. Perhaps, some time next winter, I shall get some one, who knows such things better than I do, to come and teach you about the human body, — your outward selves: how your eyes are formed and adapted for sight; and your ears for hearing; and your stomach for digestion. Who will like to hear this? All held up their hands. Which do you think you should like best, to hear about the construction of your bodies, or about your spirits? Spirits. You prefer to talk of inward things rather than outward things? Yes. Who think the analysis has taught you a good deal about yourselves? All. Who think it has taught you a good deal about the meaning of words? All. I intend you shall learn outward things too: I shall get people to come and tell you about many outward things, which I do not know much about myself. I can teach better about the inward things. Next quarter I am going to teach you about inward things, not in yourselves, but in another, — a Perfect Being. In Jesus Christ? asked some. Yes: we will study Jesus Christ; how many will be glad to do this? They all held up their hands.* How many have learned something from the analysis, — they are very sure, they know it? Almost all held up their hands. How many are sorry these lessons are over? Several. Some said they were glad the next subject was coming.

* These were the Conversations on the Gospels, subsequently published in two volumes. A selection of the best of these conversations, in an edition of one volume, is called for now.

IV.

CONCLUSION.

IN the first edition of this work, I introduced a chapter on the General Principles of Education, with an attempt to answer the question whether the human germ of never-ending existence be matter, — insensate, unthinking, involuntary, finite, lifeless matter; of which sensation, thought, volition, are mere modes, like form; or results of motion, like sound; and to which the Creator may superadd, as an attribute, eternal life. Or if it be, of itself, LIFE, from the fountain of life; feeling, thinking, willing, acting, by the same necessity of nature by which God loves, knows, creates; and to which matter is but a temporary accident.

It was rather hazardous, perhaps presumptuous, to endeavor to give analytic definition of that portion of our consciousness which, as it comes to us not by induction from the outward, but by intuition, almost defies expression. Those who have gone most deeply into this spiritual region have never attempted to do more than approximate the subject, as it were, through an address to the imagination. But there are persons who seem to think that the action of the imagination is not the embodiment of truth, but is pure fiction.

They suppose that Socrates meant by his demon a

person who was not Socrates; that Plato meant by the soul's reminiscences pre-existent individuals, and that Christians deny the Christ when they find that salvation consists in the perfection of their own souls. If these are told that such is not the interpretation of these expressions, they straightway take the idea that then they are words without any meaning whatever. It was to this class of minds I intended to speak, and to endeavor to convey, in language which I thought would be more to their taste, the idea that the soul's very life consists in its action; that there is not, over and above the soul's life, conscience, intellect, affections, happiness, virtue, salvation, — but that the soul has its substantial existence in these various modes and degrees of action, and that to educate the soul is to make common cause with its action; to think, love, hope, desire, in short, live in companionship with it.

But some to whom I wished to speak find no meaning in my words; and others smile at what seems to them the absurdity of attempting to reach a class of minds that will not take the trouble to find out within themselves what Socrates, Plato, and Jesus meant by their beautiful emblems. With the latter class of critics, I am myself inclined to agree; and confess that I should not have attempted, with my small powers, to depart from the symbolical expression, which the wise of all ages have agreed to be the only appropriate mode of conveying spiritual facts; and have gone into the shallows of analytic definition.

But as I feel no less confidence than ever in the truths

which I there attempted to explain, on omitting this chapter, whose expressions are judged on all hands to be so inadequate, I will make another effort to convey my ideas, by inserting in its place part of a conversation that I once held with a class of children under fourteen years of age, in a charity Sunday school, which did not seem to be a failure at the time; and which contains, perhaps, the whole *practical* philosophy of the matter.

I began with what is to me a very natural question when beginning to instruct in Sunday school: —

What is a soul?

It is what thinks, replied a child of eight years.

Has a little baby, just born, any soul?

Little babies must have souls, or they would not go to heaven when they die, said all.

Well, what is the soul of a baby; is it what thinks; or is it thin stuff, something like vapor or air; or is it — feelings? I spoke this question very deliberately.

Feelings, said all with decision.

What feelings — what kind of feelings has a baby?

Happy feelings, said a sweet child of ten years old.

Yes, happiness; and is there nothing else? does not a baby seem to wish to be loved, and does it not seem to love?

Yes, it is *loving;* and that is one reason it is happy.

But does a baby believe any thing?

It does not know any thing to believe, said one.

We are not sure of that: don't you remember Jesus

Christ said, "Their angels always behold the face of my Father in heaven"? Perhaps they know God!*

Babies seem to believe, said another, that people will be kind to them and love them.

You know a baby's soul, after it comes into the body, seems to lie still and enjoy itself, — i.e., its happiness, love, and faith for a good while, — but at last it begins to look out of its eyes, to see people and things about it.

It seems to have confidence in every thing, said one.

Yes: faith grows out of love and happiness. But does it know about people and things out of itself, so as to choose right in loving and having confidence?

No.

Do not some things seem to disappoint it?

Yes.

Perhaps it judges by what it feels within, and when it does not find love and happiness outside as well as within, it gets pain and terror: are all people worthy of love and confidence?

No.

And the baby may make mistakes?

Yes.

Does it know what will make it happy?

No.

How does it find out?

After a pause, one replied: Sometimes it does not find out.

* This — as I have since heard — is the first postulate of the philosophy of Gioberti; and hence perhaps his works were put on the Index by the Pope.

Very true; it is the work of life to find out: have you found out?

This home question silenced them, and I asked: Do you think, if you had always been treated with love, and always had thought others were trying to make you happy, you should ever have been discontented, or have feared or have disliked anybody?

No, said all.

Discontent then, and fear and hate, were no part of your soul at first?

No.

And if you should lose all such feelings, would it destroy your soul?

No: it would make it better; as good as it was at first.

Well, now tell me, do you think it is possible that you should lose all your desire of being loved, and all your love, all your happiness, and desire or even expectations of happiness?

After a pause for thought, they decided unanimously that they could not.

But you might lose your bad feelings, and your soul would be left?

Yes.

Then your love, happiness, and faith are your soul itself?

Yes.

And discontent, hatred, fear, do not seem to be your soul itself, but disorders and diseases of your soul?

Yes.

Each of you began, like any other little babies, with being happy, loving, and believing: have you ever made any mistakes; loved what could not love you; desired what could not make you happy; believed what was not true?

Yes, a thousand times, said several.

Will not a person who constantly makes these mistakes at last grow discontented, unloving, fearful, and full of doubts?

Yes.

And cannot you imagine a soul that seeks for happiness in so many wrong ways that after a while it becomes discouraged?

Yes.

And supposing a person loves one bad person after another, and finds them out, one by one, to be bad: don't you think, at last, he will doubt whether there is goodness anywhere?

We know God is good.

How do we know that God is good?

The Bible says so.

How did the Bible people find it out?

God told them.

How? was it in the same way as Christ says, their angels beheld the Father when they were babies? He says in another place, "The pure in heart see God."

I do not remember of seeing God, said one.

Not the form or image of God, which you have in your imagination now perhaps; and not the name of God, which you certainly did not know till you began to use your ears; but you may have *felt his character*, and it was that, perhaps, that made your first feelings happy, loving, and confidential. Your feelings remember God, for you are very sure God is good; and that is a very different thing from your head's remembering a name. Conscience, hope, and the ideals of the imagination, that "spring eternal in the human breast," are the remembrance of God's character. I dare say when you act according to conscience you feel all is right, and as if you had got home again to God, after being away.

This conversation was applied to their duties. They all had the care of infants and little children, although they were themselves so young; for thus it is in the families of the poor, when parents are obliged to go out to work. Adverting to what they had said, of babies seeming to expect people would be kind to them and love them, I remarked how different babies were in this respect from animals, who began with being afraid of every thing; and I remarked that if babies did "behold the Father," it was no wonder they believed in kindness and love; had confidence and faith in others; and that it was so long before a child could get so completely frightened by its pains that its faith would not kindle up at a smile, which is God's image in the face. They all recognized the fact that babies do not begin to be afraid until they are many months old, unless they have a great deal of pain; and they seemed to take the idea very completely, of how important it must be to watch them, when they could not speak, in order to understand what influence we were having over their little minds; and how careful we ought to be, that they should not suffer from neglect and carelessness before they could think or understand, lest doubt and fear should take the place of love and faith in their dispositions. I told them anecdotes of children who used to cry unaccountably; of one who was found, after many months, to have been afraid of the *rough feel* of broadcloth; and another, of whatever was black ; and how a wise care and tenderness should see that the little soul be not exposed to distress and shocks, which might lay the foundations of feeble-mindedness, scepticism, and fear of the unknown: but how every thing should be done to strengthen and cherish that feeling of God's character, without which it would be of no use to know God's name.

It may seem to some persons rather out of place to bring philosophy to bear upon taking care of babies. But here is the starting point of education. And Mr. Alcott does not disdain to let his thoughts begin at the beginning; since so did Christ. "Whosoever offendeth one of these little ones, it were better for him that a millstone were hung about his neck, and he were cast into the uttermost depths of the sea." The principles growing out of the few primal facts of human nature, which are stated above, carried out into the whole education, — this is Mr. Alcott's system. He would teach children to discriminate spiritual happiness from that bodily ease and enjoyment which too often takes its place; to cherish the principle of love, by feeding it on beauty and good, and not on illusion; and to clarify and strengthen faith, by getting knowledge in the right way, — not by accumulation, but by growth. For there is something at the foundation of the human soul analogous to the organization of a plant, which does indeed feed on the earth from which it springs, the air in which it flourishes, the light of heaven which comes upon it from afar; but which admits nothing that it cannot assimilate to itself. We may assist a plant if we will study its nature; but there are things which might be put round one plant which would destroy another. And so we may assist a soul; but there is only one way. We must study its nature; we must offer the individual those elements alone which it needs, and at the time it needs them, and never too much, and always enough. Then we shall find that each soul has a form, a beauty, a purpose of its own. And we shall also find that there are a few general conditions never to be shut out: that, as the light of heaven, the warmth of earth, and space to expand, are necessary to the plants, — so knowledge of God, the sympathy of human love, and liberty to act from within outward, are indispensable to the soul.

V.

EXPLANATORY.*

TO contemplate spirit in the Infinite Being has ever been acknowledged to be the ground of true religion. To contemplate spirit in external nature is universally allowed to be the true science. To contemplate spirit in ourselves, and in our fellow-men, is obviously the means of understanding social duty, and quickening within ourselves a wise humanity. In general terms, contemplation of spirit is the first principle of human culture, the foundation of self-education.

This principle Mr. Alcott begins with applying to the education of the youngest children, considering early education as a leading of the young mind to self-education.

But it is not pretended that it is peculiar to the system of education developed in the succeeding pages to aim at the contemplation of spirit, at least in theory. But perhaps it will be admitted that Mr. Alcott is somewhat peculiar in the faith which he puts in this principle, or in his fearless and persevering application of it, and especially in his not setting the child to look

* As my attempt to explain the general principles of Mr. Alcott's system in the first edition did not succeed, I made an Explanatory Preface to the second edition, which I here insert as the last chapter.

for spirit, *first*, in the vast and varied field of external nature, as seems to be the sole aim of common education. For in common education, as is well known, the attention is primarily and principally directed to the part of language which consists of the names of outward things; as well as to books which scientifically class and explain them, or which narrate events in a matter-of-fact manner.

One would think that there has been proof enough that this common plan is a bad one, in the universally acknowledged difficulty of making children study those things to which they are first put, without artificial stimulus; also in the absolute determination with which so many fine minds turn aside from word-knowledge and dry science, to play and fun, and to whatever interests the imagination or heart; and, finally, in the very small amount of acquisition which, after all the pains taken, is generally laid up, from school-days. Besides, is it not *a priori* absurd? Is not external nature altogether too vast a field for the eye of childhood to command? And is it not impossible for the mind to discover the spirit in unity, unless the field is, as it were, commanded? The result of the attempt has generally been that no spiritual culture has taken place at school. In most cases, the attention has been bewildered, discouraged, or dissipated by a variety of objects; and in the best cases the mind has become one-sided and narrow, by being confined to some particular department. Naturalists are apt to be full of oddities.

Instead, therefore, of making it his aim to make children investigate external nature after spirit, Mr. Alcott leads them, in the first place, to the contemplation of spirit as it unveils itself within themselves. He thinks there is no intrinsic difficulty in doing this, inasmuch as a child can as easily perceive and name pleasure, pain, love, anger, hate, and any other exercises of soul to which himself is subjected, as he can see the objects before his eyes; and thus a living knowledge of that part of language which expresses intellectual and moral ideas, and involves the study of his own consciousness of feelings and moral law, may be gained, external nature being chiefly made use of as imagery, to express the inward life which he experiences. Connected with this self-contemplation, and constantly checking any narrowing effect of egotism or self-complacency which it may be supposed to engender, is the contemplation of God, that can so easily be associated with it. For as the word *finite* gives meaning to the word *infinite*, so the finite virtue always calls up in the mind an idea which is henceforth named and becomes an attribute of the Eternal Spirit. Thus a child, having felt what a just action is, either in himself or another, henceforth has an idea of justice, which is pure and perfect in the same ratio as he is unsophisticated; and is more and more comprehensive of particular applications as his reason unfolds. How severe and pure it often is in a child, thousands have felt.

So when a cause is named, the First Cause becomes the immediate object of inquiry. Who taught the hen to lay its egg? said a little boy to his mother. The hen's mother, was the reply. Who taught the hen's mother? That mother had a mother. But who taught the first hen that ever laid an egg in the world? he exclaimed impatiently. This child had never heard of God. What mother or nurse will not recognize that this is the way children talk? It is proverbial that children ask questions so deep that they cannot be answered. The perception of the finite seems with them to be followed immediately by a plunge into the infinite. A wise observer will see this, even through the broken language of infancy, and often through its voiceless silence. And a deep reasoner on such facts will see that a plan of education founded on the idea of studying spirit in their own consciousness, and in God, is one that will meet children just where they are, much more than will the common plan of pursuing the laws of Nature, as exhibited in movements of the external world.

But some say that the philosophy of the spirit is a disputed philosophy; that the questions — what are its earliest manifestations upon earth, and what are the means and laws of its growth — are unsettled; and therefore it is not a subject for dogmatic teaching.

Mr. Alcott replies to this objection that his teaching is not dogmatic; that nothing more is assumed by him than that spirit exists, bearing a relation to the body in which it is manifested analogous to the relation which God bears to the external creation. And it is only those persons who are spiritual so far as to admit this, whom he expects to place children under his care.

At this point his dogmatic teaching ends; and here he takes up the Socratic mode. He begins with asking questions upon the meanings of the words which the children use in speaking, and which they find in their spelling-lessons, requiring illustrations of them in sentences composed or remembered. This involves the study of spirit. He one day began with the youngest of thirty scholars to ask illustrations of the word *brute;* and there were but three literal answers. A brute was a man who killed another; a drunken man; a man who beat his wife; a man without any love; but it was always a man. In one instance it was a boy beating a dog. Which is the brute, said Mr. Alcott, the boy or the dog? The boy, said the little girl, with the gravest face. This case indicates a general tendency of childhood, and is an opening therefore for speaking of the outward as the sign of the inward, and for making all the reading and spelling lessons exercises for defining and illustrating words. The lessons on language, given in the Record, have generally been admitted to be most valuable. Most persons seem to be struck with the advantages necessarily to be derived from the habit of inquiring into the history of words from their material origin, and throughout the spiritual applications of them which the imagination makes.

It is true that one person, in leading such an exercise, may sometimes give a cast to the whole inquiry, through the influence of his own idiosyncrasies and favorite doctrines; and Mr. Alcott's definitions may not be defensible in every instance. I am not myself prepared to say that I entirely trust his associations. But he is so successful in arousing the activity of the children's own minds, and he gives such free scope to their associations, that his personal peculiarities are likely to have much less influence than those of most instructors. Not by any means so much objection could be made to his school on this account as can be made to Johnson's Dictionary; for the manner in which the words are studied and talked about in school is such that the children must be perpetually reminded that nothing connected with spiritual subjects can be finally settled into any irreversible formula of doctrine, by finite and unperfected minds; excepting, perhaps, the two moral precepts, on which hang the law and the prophets.

Some objections have been made, however, to the questionings upon consciousness, of which specimens are given in the lessons on self-analysis. It is said that their general tendency must be to produce egotism. This might be, if, in self-analysis, a perfect standard were not always kept before the mind by constant reference to Jesus Christ as the "truth of our nature;" and by means of that generalizing tendency, which I have noticed before, which always makes children go from finite virtue to the idea of the perfect. We have found the general influence of the lessons on self-analysis to be humbling to the self-conceited and vain, though they have also encouraged and raised up the depressed and timid in one or two instances. The objection seems to me to have arisen from taking the word *self* in a too limited signification. The spirit within is what is meant by *self*, when considered as an object of philosophical investigation. I think that the lessons would more appropriately have been styled analysis of human nature than self-analysis; for, excepting the first one, they were of a very general character, and constantly became more so, in their progress. Yet the impression of that first lesson is very probably the strongest on the mind of many readers. It consisted of a series of questions, calculated to bring out the strongest and most delicate sentiments of the individual soul. Testing questions were asked, which placed the child in the painful alternative of claiming the spirit of martyrdom, or denying her sincere affections for beloved friends. I believe there was no untruth told, and no self-exaltation felt, and consequently no harm done, in the particular instance; but I will admit that it was too much an analysis of the individual, and should certainly agree with those who think that the effect of such a course might ultimately be to dwarf or dissipate, and perhaps to corrupt them, by forcing an expression of sentiments strictly personal. If there is one object more than another to which may be applied Wordsworth's beautiful lines, —

> "Our meddling intellect
> Misshapes the beauteous forms of things,
> We murder to dissect,"

it is to the personalities of the soul.

The instinctive delicacy with which children veil their deepest thoughts of love and tenderness for relatives, and their reasonable self-gratulations, should not be violated, I think, in order to gain knowledge, or for any imagined benefit to others. Indeed, no knowledge can be gained in this way. It would be as wise to tear the rosebud open, or invade the solitude of the chrysalis, with the hope of obtaining insight into the process of bloom or metamorphosis, as to expect to gain any knowledge of the soul by drawing forth, by the personal power which an instructor may possess over the heart, conscience, or imagination, that confidence which it is the precious prerogative of an individual to bestow spontaneously when old enough to choose its depository. And Mr. Alcott, I believe, agrees with me in this, notwithstanding that he practically goes sometimes upon the very verge of the rights of reserve, as in the instance referred to. He doubted immediately whether that first lesson was wise, and materially changed the character of his questioning afterwards; and an attentive reader will observe that questions of the same kind were not repeated after the first day. But I felt bound in conscience to put into the Record every thing that transpired during that winter, and to present even the exercises that were afterwards modified; because I had called my book the Record of the actual School. I expected, however, that it would be read in the liberal spirit a work on such a plan required; and that the general character of the exercises would be regarded, rather than the peculiarities of any one lesson, and especially of an introductory one, on entirely new ground.

But what I have said of the rights of reserve does not respect all that is in the soul. There are relations and sentiments which regard objects of common interest to all souls; such as God, Jesus Christ, the human race as such, and duties in the abstract. These are fair subjects of questioning, with the affections appertaining to them, and there is a great good, which may arise from the consciousness of these sentiments in each individual being analyzed and discriminated, and the relations themselves being discussed in a large company, all of whom share them, and the duties which spring from them. For so all narrowness and peculiar associations have a chance to be exchanged for something more enlarged, and the clearer reason of some may aid the dimmer apprehension of others, less favored by nature or education. And, in this case, there is no fear, as has sometimes been suggested, of the mind's being dwarfed. It may and will take narrow views, comparatively with Truth itself; but the danger is less, if this subject is first apprehended in childhood, than if it is approached for the first time at a later age. For in childhood the sense of Justice, and the sentiment of the Good and Beautiful, have not yet lost the holiness and divine balance of innocence, or the glow and impulse first received from the Divine Being, who projected the individual soul into time and space, there to clothe itself with garments, by which it may see itself, and be seen by its fellow-beings.

This view of childhood's comprehension is confirmed by all who have had much to do with cultivating the minds of children. Madame Neckar de Saussure, in her work on "Progressive Education," says that the younger children are, the more exclusively they are moral beings; a position which she defends with much fine remark, replete with her usual practical good sense. The phrenologists declare that conscientiousness is, generally speaking, larger in proportion in children than in adults (what a satire is this fact, if it be a fact, on our modes of education!); and, lastly, Jesus Christ always spoke of childhood as having peculiar moral sympathies; being of the kingdom of heaven, &c.

There is, however, one way in which there is some danger of dwarfing the minds of children on these subjects. It is this: As it is sometimes necessary to imagine or refer to practical applications of principles, and to outward occasions of sentiments, in order to identify them, we are liable to present cases which are not entirely comprehensible by children who can perfectly realize the principle or sentiment, either in their own consciousness, or in application to a case whose terms they do understand. And Mr. Alcott may sometimes err in selecting his instances of application. But I think it is very rarely that he does.

The contemplation of spirit in God is necessarily wrapt up in a study of language, leading to the study of the soul, whose existence, sentiments, reason, and strength of will are God's gifts of spirit. But Mr. Alcott did not intend to confine himself to such allusions to Jesus Christ as are found in the Record. Having arranged the four Gospels into a continuous story, to illustrate the career of spirit on earth, he read them with conversations; and he expects to prove that this mode of studying spirit is peculiarly within the reach of childhood, and particularly congenial to its holy instincts, strong sympathies, ready imagination, and unsophisticated reason. In this, as in all his other questionings, his plan is a perfectly liberal one. After reading the lesson for the day, he asks for their own associations with words, their impressions of events, the action of their imagination, and the conclusions of their reason upon them. All sides of every subject are presented by the various children, and dwelt upon, at least until they are fully expressed; and there the subject is left, Mr. Alcott making no further decision upon what is said than can be derived from the paraphrase with which he generally closes, and which he makes on the impulse of the moment. He does not wish the children to think that the meaning of Scripture is a matter of authority; and this is the chief reason why he does not decide in favor of particular views, dogmatically. He thinks it is enough to start the mind on some subjects, to "wake the echo that will not sleep again," and lays out to guard them from error, rather by the general influences of his moral and intellectual discipline than by giving them the formulas of any creed. So successful has he proved to be, in avoiding controverted points, and keeping free from the technology of sect, that one day, when two ladies — one a Trinitarian, and the other a Humanitarian — were present at a lesson on the first chapter of John, each left the room, saying to Mr. Alcott, "I perceive that my views are taught here."

Before dismissing this part of the subject, however, let me notice one thing, which is very extensively said; namely, that Mr. Alcott goes further, in his dogmatics, than to teach the existence of spirit in that relation to the body which the Deity holds to the creation; for that he teaches the Oriental doctrine of pre-existence and emanation.

But this is not the case. Mr. Alcott indeed believes that birth is a spiritual act and fact prior to embodiment. And does not every one believe this, who does not think the soul of an individual the temperament of a body, the effect of matter? For my own part, I believe that this is the only way of conceiving the unity of a spirit; and that it is the pre-existence meant in Wordsworth's ode on Immortality, and that which Plato himself meant to teach; and that it certainly is the doctrine of Christianity taught by Jesus Christ. But even this doctrine Mr. Alcott has never taught dogmatically. It has come out spontaneously from the children themselves, and, almost invariably, as soon as they come to see the divine nature of the conscience and the sentiments. It is entirely against the spirit of Mr. Alcott's plan to dogmatize even on what he believes. Some of the children have expressed a materialistic theory, and I would venture to say that they have never thought with which sect, if any, Mr. Alcott agrees, so entirely Socratic is his method of instruction.

Indeed, it is almost impossible for one who has not been in the school to understand how truly the opinion of others, even that of Mr. Alcott, becomes a secondary object of attention, after the mind has been opened into the region of ideas through consciousness, by the key of well-understood words. There is real intellectual activity in these little minds, and a pursuit of truth on the true principles. This is the case, before it is evidenced by ready answers. It often happens that a child is some weeks, and even months or a year, at school, without saying many things; but perfectly absorbed and attentive, and giving a silent vote on all questions so decided: at last he begins to speak, and almost astonishes us by his thoughts and expressions. The journals which the children begin to keep, as soon as they can join letters, also often give indications of attention and interest before there is much said. Mr. Alcott requires from all undivided attention; excepting from a small class, consisting of those who do not join in the general exercises, but sit at a side desk, and read, draw, and look at pictures, while he attends to the large class.

It will be granted that the general influence of studying language, consciousness, and the life of Christ, for the manifestations of spirit, must be favorable to moral culture, unless there is something very forced about it; and the Record of a School will probably convince any impartial reader that it can be done very easily and naturally by such an instructor as Mr. Alcott. Speculating and talking about the moral nature has, of itself, a tendency to place it uppermost in the mind; since there is an inward feeling, which raises the moral part of our nature above the intellectual and instinctive, whenever they are all brought into comparison. But this is not enough; especially where there is no dogmatic teaching. Thought should ever be accompanied with appropriate action. Mr. Alcott rests his chief dependence for the moral culture of his pupils upon the moral discipline to which he subjects them. He makes every day's duties the means of illustrating every day's speculations; and *vice versa.*

But some of his methods of discipline have been questioned. Before I had had an opportunity of observing their operation with my own eyes, I was myself much inclined to question some of them; and perhaps it will be the best means of doing both him and myself justice, to relate my own views upon this subject, and the modifications they have undergone since I have been a spectator of his School.

I will begin with saying that I have no doubt at all that, so far as regards this particular school, the methods have been in every respect salutary, and the best possible for the members of it. General intelligence, order, self-control, and good-will have been produced to a degree that is marvellous to see; especially when we consider that his scholars' ages range from three years to twelve, and none are older, and most of them only eight or nine years old.

Mr. Alcott thinks a common conscience is to be cultivated in a school, and that this will be higher in all, than any one conscience would be, if it were private. I have thought the opposite, and, pursuing my own idea in my own school, my method has, in theory, been this. I have begun with every individual, by taking it for granted, in the first place, that there is a predominating sense of duty. This is not artificial on my part; for the germ of the principle of duty lies in every mind, I know; and generally it is accompanied by a wish, at least, to follow duty. With this I would sympathize, and let my sympathy be felt, by showing my scholars that I can find the wish out, even when enveloped in many shadows. All derelictions from duty I would meet with surprise, as accidental mistakes or indisputable misfortunes, according as the fact might be; and offer my advice, endeavoring to win a confidential exposure of the individual's own moral condition, as it appears to themselves, in order that I might wisely and tenderly give suitable advice. Thus would I establish a separate understanding with each particular scholar, and act the part of a religious friend to each; while in general assembly no reference should be made to any moral wrong-doing of any one, but it be courteously and charitably taken for granted that all mean to act conscientiously and religiously.

This plan is of very fine influence, in many respects. Its tendency is to break up that odious combat which seems to go on in many schools, where there is a struggle, as it were, for power; the children trying how far they can do wrong with impunity, and the teachers constantly feeling obliged to keep on a watch, in order to preserve their prerogative. Instead of this, it introduces a sentiment of discipleship, in which the contest is, who shall be beforehand, — the pupils in yielding a willing obedience, or the teachers in giving those parental tokens which insure this *willing obedience.*

Another tendency, no less salutary, is to produce a tender and respectful courtesy in the pupils towards each other. Conscious of being engaged in the same moral course, of being assisted and inspired by the mind of the same respected friend, who only brings them to think of each other on those points of the character of each where there may be sympathy and understanding, they are not obliged to know any thing of one another which is not a ground of respect, or at least of moral interest.

This method also tends to preserve all the delicate individualities of character, and to give appropriate and differing atmosphere and scope to those flowers of delicacy and of sensibility which, like the violets of the landscape, are sunbeams in the shady places of private life. In this connection I would also observe that nothing will so effectually preserve the soul from habits of secrecy and undue reserve, as culture of the individual, as such; for nothing is so favorable to frank, open, unsuspicious transparency of soul, expressed in look and manner, as never to have been wounded, or ridiculed, or unjustly regarded, during that impressible season of life when self-estimation is first forming. The human being was made, like every thing in the creation of God, for expression. To be cherished and helped forward, by the respectful tenderness and generous liberality of mind of the guardians and companions of its infancy, involves no danger of producing that folding up of the soul within itself which is too often the disease of those who have within them what it would be a delight and a benefit for all their race to know. This disease, we shall find, is most frequent in those who have been put for education into some common mill, whence nothing can come out without bearing some particular stamp and superscription, and where of course all individualities, all that springs from the wonderful depths of personality, are rigorously worn off, or driven in. A delicate nature, in such a situation, is another form of a fact I have seen in some work on natural history; where it is said that the plants which grow so large and beautiful in the tropical regions, and come out from the beginning in a bud consisting merely of a naked fold, when transplanted to a cold climate, become dwarfed, many leaflets being arrested in their growth, and forced to degenerate into scales, in order to protect from the atmosphere the growth of the interior leaves, that the whole may not perish. So, in the ungenial atmosphere of unsympathizing guardianship or companionship, a part of the mental powers, intended to spread forth in beauty and fragrance, are forced to degenerate into mere self-defences, that all may not be lost. A fastidious reserve, where it is not affectation, is always the effect of want of sympathy and intelligent appreciation, or of a forced intercourse with the rude; and it never comes from the respectfulness of the method of education which I am defending, but is prevented by it; provided this method is pursued with good sense on the part of the instructor.

The last good influence which I shall mention, of my favorite mode of procedure, is its tendency to break up that constant reference to general opinion, which is so apt to degenerate into subserviency to it. The mind that is accustomed to commune in silence with its own ideal is apt to forget the low views which govern the world; and by this forgetfulness to be withdrawn from the world's detoning influences. The soul, also, feeling how far off it is from its own standard, even in its best estate, may be entirely unconscious of how beautiful and how elevated it appears to those around it; and thus become more and more humble, have more and more of the "beauty of contrition" about it, as it advances. And what expression is there on earth, of the unseen and unknown heaven of character to which we all aspire, that is so powerful as the unconsciousness and humility of the holiest virtue?

But while I bear testimony to having found that this method of individual culture can be pursued in a school, and with all the above fine influences, I must be ingenuous, and also state its peculiar difficulties.

It requires, in the first place, that the school be small in numbers; for no instructor can take time to study out the individualities of every pupil, and feed each with appropriate food, without a greater tax upon thought and feeling than any individual can bear for many successive years. It requires, also, that the instructor should be free for the school, so as to make it the first object; and free also for general culture, and for such degree of general intercourse as there is felt a need for. It is not every well-disposed or well-taught person who is capable of the attitude of friend and guardian to a company of young minds. It requires, even more than much learning, a spirit of philosophic liberality, a mind of ready and various resource, and a heart of all-comprehending sympathies.

But supposing the instructor is found, and the school is numerically within compass, it will often take years to get entire possession of some individuals who may come into it, the general influences of whose life and companionship out of school may not be in harmony with the influence exerted by the instructor. Where so much is aimed at, relative success alone must be expected; and an instructor must not be surprised if every degree of want of success makes a great noise in the world, and there be little appreciation of the success actually obtained, except by the pupils themselves, who will inevitably feel and acknowledge it as they grow older.

When I went into Mr. Alcott's school, full of the above views, and rather inclined to believe that the method I had endeavored to pursue was the only one that was not absolutely wrong, my mind was forcibly turned to consider other modes.

Here was a school of thirty children, mostly boys under ten years of age, who were creatures of instinct more than any thing else, with undeveloped consciences and minds; but well-disposed, good-natured, and overflowing with animal spirits, and all but intoxicated with play. It was plain enough that my plan could get no foothold in a school of such materials; at least until some other one had prepared the way. And I soon found that Mr. Alcott had quite a different way. A common conscience was the first object towards which he aimed. And this he defended on the ground that the general conscience of a school would be the highest; for which, also, he had some very excellent arguments. He said that the soul when nearest infancy was the purest and most moral; that the artlessness of children made them express their strongest convictions, even when it made against themselves; and that though the very young were very apt to do wrong things, they did not defend wrong in the abstract. From all this, it was to be inferred that the moral judgments of the majority would be higher than their conduct; while those few, whose conduct was more in proportion to their moral judgment, would still keep their high place, and occasionally throw their finer elements into the general conscience, which might be called the treasury of the school. I admitted the reasonableness of all this, and felt that the plan would work for the benefit of the worst scholars, certainly, and might work for the benefit of the best; and I am bound to say that no evil effects to the better portion have transpired under my observation, quickened though it has been by my doubts; and that the majority of the school have made moral progress, which, considering their age, and the time that has transpired, is beyond all parallel in my observation. I say *moral* progress, and I wish to be understood in the largest sense of that word; in which are included religious ideas, the sense of accountability, and the habit of virtuous effort. I therefore must acknowledge myself vanquished, so far as my scepticism regarded such a school as Mr. Alcott's; though I reserve my own opinion respecting one of a very limited number of girls, of an age extending from the time they can read to the time when girls generally leave school. As it is the ideal of a girl's education to be educated by an accomplished mother, in the sacred retreat of home, the nearest approach to these circumstances is the ideal of a girl's school.

The methods of discipline which I mentioned as having been questioned, all arise out of this principle of having a common conscience; and these objections I will now briefly consider.

Mr A. has an office of superintendent of conduct, including attitude, appearances of inattention, &c. This is delegated to scholars, selected for the day, whom sometimes he chooses himself, and sometimes the scholars choose, and to whom the whole always agree, promising to submit without complaint to any punishments Mr. Alcott may found on their judgments; experience having proved to them that this office generally creates that sense of responsibility which makes the marks strictly just, especially as they know that Mr. Alcott always reserves a right of judgment, over and above that of the superintendents. Of this office, I was very jealous at first. I predicted various evils. But the result has proved that Mr. Alcott was right in expecting from it excellent effects. The worst boys, when put into that office, become scrupulously just, and get an idea of superintending themselves, which nothing else can give them.

General discussion of the conduct of individual scholars is also another method of discipline, arising out of the principle of forming a common conscience. The objections to this course are obvious; and I have felt some, though not those usually urged. And, with respect to the objections I made, I cannot say that any positive evil has been done, while I must admit that positive good does certainly arise. A degree of honesty, simplicity, self-surrender, and general acknowledgment of a standard of action beyond the control of any individual, are produced, such as no other school in the land, I will venture to say, can show; while all false pretensions, vanity, and self-exaltation are completely taken down. Some persons have thought vanity was cherished in the school; but I think there can be no greater mistake. The first display of a new scholar is that of all his vanity, and this is so uniformly the case that the development is quite amusing to a constant spectator. But this blossom is indeed short-lived. It soon falls, and the germ of a sober estimate of himself appears. In short, there can be no doubt at all that the immediate effect of this part of Mr. Alcott's plan is favorable to self-knowledge and humility, when the scholars compare themselves with one another. It has been said that the children are vain of the school, and think it the only place where the right method is pursued, and that they are the only persons in the world who have the right standard, &c. A sort of party spirit about a school is not uncommon with children, especially when there is any thing peculiar in the school. And if this is stronger than usual in this instance, it must be said, in defence of the children, that they often hear the most absurd misrepresentations of it, and of Mr. Alcott, from people who judge without knowing the truth; and the wildest criticisms and inquiries concerning it, from those who are inclined to take marvellous views of it. They often tell Mr. Alcott that people do not understand him or his school. And this is perfectly true. However, let the case be as it may, if the children overrate the school while they are in it, they are so much more liable to receive all its advantages; and they will soon be undeceived after they have left it.

Having spoken thus elaborately of the school, with respect to its principles and methods of moral culture, I will proceed to speak of it with respect to its intellectual effects; and here, I for one have never had any doubts in any particular. I think it can be proved *a priori* and *a posteriori* that the intellectual influences are in all respects salutary.

In the first place, the cultivation of attention as a moral duty, with the constant exposition of all which interferes with it in instinctive habits, is of the first importance to the intellectual life. The mode in which this state of mind is cultivated is not merely that of stating it as a duty, but stating it as a duty after having used all the resources of his own and others' genius to attract and reward their attention. When a child has been led to enjoy his intellectual life in any way, and then is made to observe whence his enjoyment has arisen, he can feel and understand the argument of duty which may be urged in favor of attention. Those who commonly instruct children would be astonished to witness the degree of attention which Mr. Alcott succeeds in obtaining from his scholars constantly. Indeed the majority of adults might envy them. It is, generally speaking, complete, profound, and as continuous as any would wish the attention of children to be.

The first object of investigation is also in the highest degree fruitful for the intellect. Spirit as it appears within themselves, whether in the form of feeling, law, or thought, is universally interesting. No subject interests children so much as self-analysis. To give name to inward movements of heart and mind, whether in themselves or others, is an employment of their faculties which will enchain the attention of the most volatile. There is no one class of objects in external Nature which interests all children; for children are very differently gifted with respect to their sympathies with Nature. But all are conscious of something within themselves which moves, thinks, and feels; and as a mere subject of curiosity, and of investigation for the sake of knowledge, it may take place of all others. In order to investigate it, a great many things must be done which are in themselves very agreeable. Mr. Alcott reads and tells stories calculated to excite various moral emotions. On these stories he asks questions, in order to bring out from each, in words, the feelings which have been called forth. These feelings receive their name and history and place in the moral scale. Then books and passages from books are read, calculated to exercise various intellectual faculties, such as perception, imagination, judgment, reason, conscience; and these various exercises of mind are discriminated and named. There can be no intellectual action more excellent than this, whether we consider the real exercise given to the mind, or its intrinsic interest to the children, and consequently the naturalness of the exercise. And its good influence with respect to preparing for the study of science is literally incalculable. There is not a single thing that cannot be studied with comparative ease by a child who can be taught what faculties he must use, and how they are to be brought to bear on the subject, and what influence on those faculties the subject will have after it is mastered.

But Mr. Alcott would not sequestrate children from Nature, even while this preparatory study of spirit is going on. He would be very thankful to throw all the precious influences of a country life, its rural employments, its healthful recreations, its beautiful scenery, around his scholars' minds. He thinks that the forms of Nature, as furniture for the imagination and an address to the sentiments of wonder and beauty, and also as a delight to the eye and as models for the pencil, cannot be too early presented, or too lovingly dwelt upon. In lieu of these circumstances, which of course cannot be procured in Boston, he reads to them of all in Nature which is calculated to delight the imagination and heart. He surrounds them also with statuary and pictures in his school-room; and he has drawing taught to all his scholars by a gentleman* who probably possesses the spirit of art more completely than any instructor who has ever taught in this country.

And in the lessons on words in the spelling, reading, and grammatical exercises, on which the intellectual benefits of Mr. Alcott's school are mainly based, if the spiritual part of language is dwelt on so much both as a means and as an effect of the study of the spirit within, yet the names of external objects as external, and the technical terms of art, are not necessarily excluded. A great deal of knowledge of things is conveyed in this way, and attention is more and more directed to this part of language as scholars continue at the school, and need less and less exclusive conversation on the subjects appertaining to moral discipline.

The more scientific study of Nature, also, Mr. Alcott thinks has its place in education; and he would gladly

* Mr. Francis Graeter: who has in contemplation to publish a work developing the whole art of drawing, especially from Nature, in the same way as he has often done orally to such pupils as have received the most benefit from him; and more completely than he could do in a course of desultory lessons, — more completely than has ever been done in a book for learners. We hope nothing will prevent nor delay this great desideratum *to all* lovers of the pencil.

have it pursued in his school, although the age of his scholars, together with his views as to what ought to be taught first, throw natural science out of his course, excepting what is included in the study of Language, Geography, and Arithmetic, on the plans mentioned in the Record. Is it, however, peculiar to his school, that attainments in the natural sciences are not made at the age of twelve? Will not most persons admit that, however difficult soul-analysis may be, it is still more difficult for children to seize science, which is "Nature in the abstract;" and are not the laws of the Eternal Spirit, displayed in external nature, far more abstracted from their own consciousness than are those emotions and moral laws to which Mr. Alcott so often directs their attention? There is not a little illusion on this subject of science. If children learn the names of the stars; if they gather flowers into herbariums; and stones and minerals and shells and insects into cabinets; and witness some experiments in chemistry, it is supposed that they have studied the sciences. But all this is child's play; or, at best, only useful for the healthful bodily exercise which is sometimes involved in making herbariums and cabinets. Astronomy does not consist of the heavenly bodies, but of their laws of motion and relations to each other; nor chemistry of the earthly substances of which it treats, but of their laws of combination and means of analysis. In short, nothing need be said to prove that it is absurd to attempt to teach the sciences to children under twelve years old. They should be led to Nature for the picturesque and for poetry, not for the purpose of scientific analysis and deduction. They should look upon its synthesis as sacred. The time will come when they may explore it, as God's means for aiding and completing the building up of their own intellect; and it is a positive moral injury to them to study it while they are too young to understand this object. My readers may smile, and yet it is true, that in teaching geometry I have been in the habit of so presenting it to the minds of my pupils, that fretting and passion, when occasioned by the difficulty of mastering a demonstration of those laws by which the Creator constituted the universe, could easily be checked by a single word reminding them that it was the Creator's mind we were studying. Nothing can be more blessed than the influence of this view, when connected, as it should be, with benignant views of the Deity, as the all-cherishing and all-animating Father of our spirits. Mr. Alcott says, — Let children sketch from Nature, cultivate flowers, cherish animals, keep shells and pretty stones; but defer the study of Natural Philosophy, Botany, Zoölogy, Conchology, Mineralogy, &c., till after they have learned those principles of arrangement which are to be found within the soul, and which are nearer and more easily apprehended than any natural science. And is not this rational?

Also, if Mr. Alcott does not pretend to teach the natural sciences, he does what will ultimately prove of the highest service to scientific education, in giving his scholars the habit of weighing the meaning and considering the comparative force of words. A long preparation of this kind for the study of the sciences is fully made up in the ease with which any science is mastered, by a previous knowledge of words. Time is wasted to an incalculable extent, in common education, and even in self-education, on account of our want of precision in the ideas we attach to words, which are too familiar to our ear for us to realize that we do not clearly understand them. A great effort is made to remember lessons, and then they are forgotten. Perhaps those are the soonest forgotten which it is the greatest effort to remember. But if the study is chosen with reference to the state of the mind, and the words of the lesson are perfectly understood, there need be no effort of mere memory. A clear and vivid conception, together with actual growth of mind, is remembered involuntarily. Nothing is more common than to confound intellectual labor with drill. Yet nothing can be more different than these. Bodily accomplishments, sleight of hand, &c., are attained by mere repetition; but intellectual accomplishment and acuteness are not attained by mere repetition of impression, though this is very commonly thought, but by a perfectly clear and vivid conception in the first place, dwelt upon so long that its most important relations may be developed, and not long enough to harass or weary the mind. Indeed, it is well known that repetition of the same mental impressions may destroy the memory altogether. The laws of bodily and mental discipline are precisely the reverse of each other. I could deduce a thousand facts under my own observation, to confirm this view with respect to the true culture of memory.

It is not for moral education only that self-analysis and the study of the "truth of our nature" in Jesus Christ are desirable. It is no less beneficial to the intellectual education. The soul itself, when looked on as an object, becomes a subject of scientific classification, in its faculties and operations; and the consideration of the true principles and conduct of life is most favorable to the development of right judgment, especially when parallel lives, showing approximations to the ideal, or even wanderings from it, are given in connection with the study of the life of Jesus, thus affording variety of illustration. Indeed, there is something peculiarly appropriate to the young in the study of Biography. But there is very little biography written which gives an insight into the life of the mind, and especially into its formation. It is only occasionally that we find a philosopher who can read other men's experience, and to whom the incidents of a life are transparent. But for the purposes of education there should be biographies of the childhood of genius and virtue, on the plan of Carlyle's Life of Schiller, and his articles on Burns and others.

To supply the want of biography, Mr. Alcott relies a great deal upon journal-writing, which is autobiography, while it hardly seems so to the writer. To learn to use words teaches us to appreciate their force. And, while Mr. Alcott presents this exercise as a means of self-inspection and self-knowledge, — enabling the writers to give unity to their own being by bringing all outward facts into some relation with their individuality, and gathering up fragments which would otherwise be lost, — he knows he is also assisting them in the art of composition, in a way that the rules of rhetoric would never do. Every one knows that a technical memory of words and of rules of composition gives very little command of language; while a rich consciousness, a quick imagination, and force of feeling seem to unlock the treasury: and even so vulgar a passion as anger produces eloquence, and quickens perception to the slightest inuendo.

Self-analysis, biography, and journal-writing, therefore, since they bear upon the skilful use of language, are as truly the initiation of intellectual as of moral education. And language has always professedly stood in the forefront of children's studies. The ancient languages, although they took their place in that early stage of education which they now occupy, when they were living languages, and necessary for the purpose of any reading whatever, have retained the same position, notwithstanding many disadvantages which the study of them at an early period has involved, mainly because of the good effect which has been experienced from the concentration of attention upon the vernacular words by which the Latin and Greek words are translated; and from the acquisition of the spirit of one's native tongue, by the recognition of its idioms in contra-distinction to those of other languages. It would have a much more creative influence upon the faculties of the young, besides saving much time and distress, if the study of English, on Mr. Alcott's plan, should come first; and that of the ancient languages be delayed a few years. Boys, generally speaking, would be better fitted for college at fourteen or fifteen, even in Latin and Greek, if they did not begin to learn them till they were twelve years old; always providing, however, that they thoroughly study English by means of self-analysis, poetry, and religious revelation up to that time.

Mr. Alcott, it is true, has Latin taught in his school with reference to fitting boys for the other schools; and it does not interfere with the prosecution of his own plans, since his assistant has long been in the habit of teaching it with reference to such results as he secures by his exercises on English words.

These observations on the intellectual bearings of the study of language will explain much that is peculiar in Mr. Alcott's school. And it will show that the intellectual results are never separated from the moral, and consequently never neglected. Gradually self-knowledge becomes psychology; knowledge of language, grammar; and the practice of composition leads to the true principles of rhetoric. Even if, by removal from the school, these results are not attained under his immediate observation, he cannot doubt that they will surely follow, from the principles which he sets in operation.

But I am frequently asked, Will children ever be

willing to study from books, who have been educated by Mr. Alcott? I have always answered to this question, and I will here repeat, that they will study from books more intelligently, thoroughly, and profoundly, just in proportion as they imbibe the spirit of his instructions; for they will have a clearly defined object whenever they open a book, and the beautiful things Mr. Alcott constantly reads to them have a tendency to make them feel what treasures are locked up in books. Yet they may not be bookworms. They learn that there are other sources of knowledge, and especially that thought is the chief source of wisdom. There is much illusion concerning children's reading: the book-devouring which is frequently seen nowadays in children is of no advantage to them. There is a great deal in the spirit of that maxim of Aquinas, "Read one book to be learned." Mr. Alcott's scholars may show less interest than some other children in the miserable juvenile literature which cheats so many poor little things into the idea that they know the sciences, history, biography, and the creations of the imagination; and, if it be so, it is a blessing to their minds. But many of the parents of the children have told me that they read over and over again at home the books of classical literature which he reads to them in school. And what can be finer than this effect?

Nor is the study of books excluded from the school. This is so common a mistake with respect to Mr. Alcott's plan, that perhaps I could not do better than to enter into some details respecting the precise manner in which the studying from books in its various departments is conducted. In the first place, with respect to

THE ENGLISH LANGUAGE.

As the analysis of English words into letters, and the unfolding of the meanings contained in them, constitute the foundation of an English education, spelling and defining words are the most prominent intellectual exercises of the school. The children learn the spelling-lesson by writing the given number of words on their slates, or in manuscript books, with pencils; those who do not yet write the script hand print, or endeavor to print them. The spelling-book they use is Pike's, which was selected because it contains the primitive words of the language, together with such derivatives as are roots in relation to other words. But a spelling-book containing the roots of the language, and nothing more, is yet a desideratum with us, which Mr. Alcott hopes to supply, when he gets leisure to study the Anglo-Saxon language, whence the life of our tongue undoubtedly springs.

After writing the words, the children spell them to themselves; and when they think they can arrange the letters rightly, they look out their meanings in their Johnson's Dictionaries, a copy of which is placed at each desk. They are also directed to imagine sentences in which the words can be used, or to remember any sentences which contain them, that they may have heard or read. Those who are too young to manage a bulky dictionary, Mr. Alcott orally teaches, as may be seen in the Record. Grammatical exercises, which consist of the analysis of sentences and the classification of words according to their meanings, also constitute a regular exercise. Children soon become expert in abstracting and classifying words in this way, although quite unacquainted with the technicalities of grammatical science.

And is not this the true way of beginning to study the grammar of one's native tongue? Is it not indisputable that in all sciences the principle of the classification should be understood before the nomenclature is presented? But in none is it so indispensable as in the science of grammar, whose very material requires an effort of abstraction in order to be apprehended, and whose nomenclature is rendered peculiarly hard on account of the obsolete, the foreign, and the awkwardly figurative words it contains. To the latinized scholars who first made English Grammar a science, it undoubtedly explained itself, and assisted the mind in acquisition, as the nomenclature of chemistry does. But to children of the present day it interferes with the progress of acquisition by seeming so entirely extraneous to the subject in hand. Were it not for the convenience of understanding the grammars of foreign languages, it would be better to give it all up. But since there is no other universal language of grammar, a middle course can be taken, and the English grammar may be taught according to a more lively classification and in a more lively language; and the nomenclature of Universal Grammar be taught as a separate affair. This is what Mr. Alcott endeavors to do.

GEOGRAPHY.

Geography was at first taught on Mr. Carter's plan; but as it succeeded less in interesting these children than the other lessons, we soon laid it aside, determined to think out another method which might combine more advantages; and the one adopted seemed to work well, notwithstanding we were at some disadvantage on account of the difficulty of collecting books and pictures for our purpose.

The whole school being resolved into one class, they received three conversation-lectures a week on Geography. The first three lectures consisted of a description of the solar system addressed to the picturesque imagination. They were called on to imagine themselves placed in the centre of the sun; and to picture the scene presented to the eye, supposing that organ strong enough to look through and beyond Herschel. The discipline of Mr. Alcott's readings and their good habits of attention rendered these conversations very successful, as we found when they were called on to describe the scene themselves. The forces that produce circular motion were illustrated, and thus all the astronomy which such children could well comprehend was set forth. At the third lecture, Bryant's "Song of the Stars" was read, which very much interested them as they were called to shape in their minds all the imagery.

Having given an idea of the solar system, the earth

was approached more nearly, and its atmosphere considered. They were led to imagine the clouds which hang in the atmosphere as they would appear to a person coming to our earth from another planet. And, to illustrate this, extracts were read from books describing the clouds as they appear from mountains, when they hang below the summits. Descending upon the surface of the earth, we observed on what principle it was divided into zones. And the characteristic vegetation, &c., of each zone was dwelt upon, in a lecture devoted to the purpose. The mountain scenery of the various parts of the globe was next considered; and descriptions of remarkable scenes among mountains were selected from such books of travels as we could procure, among which Humboldt's was found most interesting. Having proceeded thus far, the pupils were set to drawing the outlines of the four quarters of the globe, and required to indicate the mountainous parts.

As it is very difficult to draw these outlines, on account of their irregularity, it required repeated trials, which occupied them day after day. But it is obvious that in constantly looking upon the maps, in order to draw these outlines, a great deal will be learned from them. Warning was constantly given, however, lest the impressions on the imagination, left by the descriptions that were read, should be lost, by dwelling on such an inadequate representation of the green and flowery valleys, the snow-clad and forest-cinctured mountains, and the rock-bound coasts of the magnificent ocean, as a mere map must necessarily be. The scholars commenced drawing outlines on the black-board; but as fast as they are prepared for it, Mr. Alcott gives them manuscript books, in which they draw maps, and write whatever they can learn of the countries.

Lakes and rivers naturally come next to mountains as striking features of the earth's surface. These afford fine scope for picturesque description and illustration. The waters of our own country are so magnificent that they have attracted much attention. Flint's Valley of the Mississippi, Irving's Tour in the Prairies, occasional passages in Audubon's Ornithological Biography, &c., afford much aid to this portion of the course. Engravings and paintings too, of the river and lake scenery of many parts of the world, can be procured. When the children come to draw these lakes and rivers, of which they have seen pictures, or with which they associate scenes of human life from the journals of travellers and naturalists, they will find it much more easy to remember their names, than if they have no other idea than a mere black line may convey. It is not impossible, also, for the instructor to assist the young imagination to take bird's-eye views of the rivers and lakes of a continent, by suggesting to them to look down as from a balloon upon the earth, and see how these rivers flow from the mountains, mingle together, and find the sea.

The ocean then becomes the object of study; its proportion to the land and its general characteristics. Parts of Mr. Greenwood's article on the sea were read from the Token; and descriptions of striking sea scenes from various books, especially beautiful scenes of the tropical seas. Here some account was naturally given of the first attempts to explore the ocean; of the voyages of Columbus, and of other discoverers; and the boys were recommended to read at home Cook's Voyages. The more a human interest is thrown over external objects, the more easily they can be remembered; and therefore the narratives of voyagers are so important. Descriptions of whale-catching, seal-catching, pearl-diving, &c., were found very useful when brought into these lessons upon the ocean.

Columbus' Journal of his first voyage, which gives us beautiful descriptions of the West India Islands, and Irving's two works, were read; the intention being to give a very complete idea of all the shores of the sea. There was much difficulty, however, in obtaining information for this part of the course. It would be very convenient if a book were to be made containing a description of the coasts and harbors all over the world; and of the sea-ports, with their commercial relations. And would not this be the best practical geography for boys?

During the whole of the course, it is intended that the drawing of maps should be continued, and all the natural features of the earth indicated. The last part of geography studied should be the arbitrary divisions made by human politics. By associating this, however, with the history of nations, as the other parts of geography were associated with natural history and biography, it will be more easily remembered, and those parts of the world will be best known which it is the most important to know accurately. When these political divisions are considered, the children can draw them on their maps, and indicate the places of the towns.

Is it not obvious that geography studied in this way might put into the mind some adequate conception of the face of the earth? while the common plan fails to touch the imagination, and terminates in little more than a knowledge of maps, which is not sufficiently interesting to be retained in the memory. For it is a fact, which every thoughtful teacher must have observed, that little is permanently remembered which does not touch the heart or interest the imagination. Years are given by children to the study of geography, and yet scarcely any person retains an accurate recollection of the relations of places to each other beyond their school-days, so as to dispense with the constant use of a map. It would not be so, if the thoughts wandered over the real earth, with all its pomp and garniture, instead of being fastened to that linear hieroglyphic, the much-lauded map; which is perhaps a necessary evil, but certainly is an evil, when it precludes the mind from forming within itself a real picture of the original. Beauty and magnificence are inspirations, and secure the constant recurrence of the mind to and lingering of the thoughts over whatever fact they associate themselves with; and enable us to *learn it by heart*, — which very phrase, like most of our idioms, is full of spiritual philosophy. Why, then, should not these associations be brought to the aid of memory in attaining a knowledge of geography?

LATIN.

About a third of the school were formed into a Latin class, immediately on its commencement; and an hour a day was set apart for Latin lessons, and that portion of time was always given to it. When only three lessons a week were given, more than an hour was assigned.

They commenced by learning a portion of the Historia Sacra, with the English, thus: the first phrase was translated to the whole class, and each was called on to repeat it. By the time each, all round, had repeated it once, all had learned it by heart. At the end of each sentence, and of each paragraph, the whole was reviewed. In three months, one little girl, under seven years of age, had learned sixteen sections. Some who then began Latin, or who were absent a good deal, or were not so quick to learn, did not accomplish more than two. But all learned thoroughly all they studied, spelling and defining every word, even into the discriminations of grammar.

At the same time there were parallel lessons in grammar. They learned the paradigms of the regular conjugations, though not within the first three months; and could parse verbs in the course of six months. They also learned to discriminate the parts of speech, and had various grammatical exercises, corresponding as much as possible to Mr. Alcott's lessons in English Grammar. Besides these, some of the older, brighter, or more advanced children wrote the exercises in Leverett's Latin Tutor upon the conjugations and declensions.

It is but justice to myself, however, to state that this plan of teaching Latin was not exactly according to my own ideal; but was adopted because it was the best one that could be pursued in the circumstances, more especially with relation to the circumstance that the learners were not to be continued in Mr. Alcott's school to fit for college, but were to be removed from it to other schools, with whose methods some harmony must be kept up, for the sake of not puzzling the children. The above exercises are very good to precede the discipline of the Boston Grammar School, for instance; and will be found not an undesirable introduction to the methods pursued in that very great improvement upon classical education, — the school kept in Boston by Mr. Henry Cleveland and Mr. Edmund Cushing.

But it would be my method — a method I have myself pursued in some instances with pupils of my own school, whose education has been entirely confided to me — to wait until the pupil had been well trained in all such exercises in English as Mr. Alcott begins with, and then to commence Latin by presenting the theory of the language to the imagination.

The classical languages admit of being so presented; for they are works of art, — splendid exhibitions of the plastic genius which is manifest in every production of the Greek and Roman mind. Sound was looked upon by the Latins as a material, and the very element of air was hewn and carved into harmonious and beautiful forms, to give outness to the movements and modifications of their thought. In modern languages, words are, as it were, shapeless, elemental blocks: every modification of thought requires a separate piece to express it. The accessory and auxiliary ideas to the action and object stand around them, like the attendants on a savage king, without uniformity of dress, or trained step and air. But the Latin language may be considered the architecture of sound, the theme-syllables of the verb or the noun being the blocks of articulate air, representing the unmodified action or object, which come out of the Roman mouth defined in form as with a graver's tool, every stroke of which expresses another shade of thought. And if the accidents of these main subjects of discourse require new blocks of material, yet even these are all subordinated, and obliged to present themselves in a correspondent form to the words they qualify, or for which they stand. The communication of this theory immediately arrests the learner's mind, and fixes his attention upon those tables of terminations, which it is generally such weary work for the memory to master.

Having communicated this theory, I would, in the next place, present tables of the terminations of the verbs, choosing the most regular to begin with; but while the pupils are learning them, and those variations of meaning which they indicate, I should take some author of the Augustan age (I have sometimes begun with the Bucolics of Virgil), and teach translation by word of mouth. For I am sure it will be found that the meanings of words may be fastened on the memory by the teacher's being the dictionary a great deal more quickly and effectively than by the use of a lexicon: the animating influence of the teacher's mind, in tracing the history of the word from its material root into its imaginative applications; in associating its sound with its English derivations, whenever there are any; in opening the learner's mind to the appropriateness of the author's present application of it, which may be always shown in a real classic author; and, finally, in leading him to observe its euphonious location in the sentence, — an object so constantly kept in view by the Latin authors, whether of prose or poetry, — is all powerful to keep the acquiring mind of the learner in that cheerfulness, good-will, and vividness of imagination, which are essential to readiness and retentiveness of memory. And while, by means of the vocabulary thus attained, there may be perpetual exercises of the knowledge gained by the tables of terminations, a ground-work is forming for parsing lessons of a more philosophical character. As soon as a passage of fifty lines has been thus learned with the English meanings, the teacher must begin to explain the theory of case, and show what general relations are indicated by the several changes discriminated in the grammar by the terms nominative, genitive, dative, &c., the force of which technical words is involved in such an explanation. Then the syntactical rules should be taken up and each word explained, and the pupil required to find out, by means of the English sense (which he has learned by heart), whether any words in the passage before him afford instances of its application. If children have been well exercised, beforehand, in the analysis of English, and have learned the various force of English prepositions, the parsing of Latin substantives will be learned with great rapidity and thoroughness in this way, long before the tables of terminations are presented, — which are so great a tax to the memory, and so little assistance, after all, in determining the case of a word. These tables of terminations, however, can be given at last; and will have their use, especially as applied to the adjectives and other subordinate parts of speech.

The successful pursuit of this method requires several conditions, however. In the first place it requires previous discipline in the English language, — a discipline which, even on Mr. Alcott's method, could seldom be completed before a boy was nine years of age, if he began at six or seven. It would also require the best and freshest hours of the day; and must be the main object of the student's attention for a time, with some degree of freedom in the use of his voice to help his ear. With these conditions, there are few boys of ten or twelve years of age who might not learn so much Latin in a year as to be able to read with facility, and without farther teaching, all the Latin books preparatory to college life. Farther teaching on collateral subjects would indeed be useful; and that higher teaching might be appreciated, which consists in discriminating the characteristic styles of authors, by an observation of those relations with which his mind is most familiar, indicated by his favorite syntactical and etymological rules of construction.

ARITHMETIC.

Arithmetic was taught from the opening of the school. The younger scholars were provided with Fowle's Child's book of Arithmetic, and the older ones with Colburn's First Lessons, and learned lessons in them; though those who studied Latin had but little time for Arithmetic, and did not make any great progress.

Besides this, a course of lessons on numeration, and the fundamental rules of ciphering, were given by means of the blackboard to the whole school, in lectures. These were very useful, but it was found that, generally speaking, the children were not skilled enough in mental Arithmetic to have it any advantage to proceed further in ciphering.

GEOMETRY.

A small class in Grund's Geometry was formed also a few months after the school began. But as the children were rather young for it, and had so many other studies, it was finally laid aside, to be resumed when there is good reason for it.

COMPOSITION.

From the foregoing remarks it will be evident that book-learning is not entirely neglected by Mr. Alcott. Yet it is true that he lays himself out rather to prepare his scholars to receive it after they have left him, than to give it to them himself, at the early age when they are under his own care. His main object is to produce activity of mind, and taste for intellectual pursuits. And for the purpose of activity he uses one means which is very much neglected in common schools; and that is, he leads them to express their thoughts on paper, as soon as they can write the script hand so as to be read. Several of his pupils commenced their journals as soon as they came; but it was some time before these became any record of the inward life. The children were entirely unused to composition, and at first only set down the most dry and uninteresting circumstances. Mr. Alcott, however, contented himself with expressing the hope that by and by we should have more thoughts mingled with the record of facts; and he made no criticisms on the language, or even on the spelling; knowing that courage is easily checked, in these first efforts, by criticism; and wishing to produce a sense of freedom as a condition of free expression. He did not expect interesting views from them, until their minds were more thoroughly trained to self-inspection and inward thought. He has little reliance on any method of producing the impulse to composition, except the indirect one of leading children to think vividly and consecutively, which leads of itself to expression. And still less has he any reliance upon the power of a composition which was not the result of an inward impulse. A mere mechanical exercise leads to a tame and feeble style, which it is a misfortune to acquire, and which generates no desire to write more; but it is spontaneous to endeavor to express energetically what one feels vividly and conceives clearly: and any degree of success in this inspires ardor for new attempts.

Instructors are not, perhaps, aware how much the art of composition is kept from being developed in children, by petty criticism. Children have a great deal to contend with, in the attempt to express their thoughts. In the first place, they find it more difficult than better trained minds do, to preserve their thoughts in their memory. For the mechanical labor of holding the pen, of seeing to the spelling, of pointing, and all such details, interferes with the purely mental effort. And even when all this is mastered, and they express original thought, it is like putting out a part of themselves; and they are intensely alive to its reception, in proportion to its real originality; and if it is misunderstood, or its garb criticised, they shrink more than they would at a rude physical touch, and will be very much tempted to suppress their own thoughts, on another occasion, and only attempt the commonplaces, for which they have heard expressions.

For there seems to be in all finely attempered spirits a natural modesty, sometimes even a shrinking delicacy, which instinctively forbids exposure of the invisible exercises of the mind and heart, except to the eye of a generous liberality and a tender love; and it is only time for reflection and a fully realized faith which gives the strength of mind that may separate the sense of personality from the expression of general truth and beauty, and make clear and possible to them the duty of reposing on the intrinsic worth of what is said, and at all events frankly to express themselves.

And is there not a beautiful cause for the modesty of childhood and genius? Is not the ideal, in these instances, more vivid, to which their own actual creation is so painful a contrast that, if they are forced to attend to the discrepancy, they are discouraged? It has been remarked that the first essays of high genius are seldom in perfect taste, but exhibit "the disproportions of the ungrown giant." This can be easily explained. Genius is apt to feel most deeply the infinite, and, never losing sight of even those connections which it does not express, is unaware of the imperfections of what is seen by others, which is only a part of what is created in its own being. But if left to a natural development, and unhindered by internal moral evil, the mind always works itself out to perfect forms; while premature criticism mildews the flower, and blasts the promised fruit.

This case of genius is not irrelevant. Intellectual education, as an art, is an embodiment of all those laws and means which the development of genius manifests to be the best atmosphere for the production of creative power. For all minds are to be cherished by the same means by which genius is developed. In the first place, we never know but we have genius to deal with among our pupils, and should therefore always make our plan with reference to it; knowing that the smallest degree of mind is also benefited in its due proportion by the discipline which brings out the highest, and is certainly quenched by those processes from which genius suffers. It would not perhaps be going too far to say that the period of school education is too early a period for criticism on any original production. There is only one fault which may be excepted from this rule, and that is affectation; a style which proceeds from want of the sentiment of truth. Even this, however, should not be taken up as a literary blunder, but as moral evil, of which it is an expression, quite as much as affectation of manners, and want of veracity.

The objections made against the intellectual influences of Mr. Alcott's school, by those who do not know much about it, are chiefly of the negative character, which the foregoing pages have attempted to answer. There is one, however, of a positive character, on which I wish to make some observations, and then I shall close this protracted essay.

It is said that Mr. Alcott cultivates the imagination of his scholars, inordinately, by leading them to the works of the poets, and to the prose creations of such writers as Krummacher, Bunyan, Carova, &c. It is thought that by exercising the minds of the children in following authors of this class; requiring them to picture out all the imagery of their language; and leading them to consider, also, the inward life which this imagery is intended to symbolize, the energy of the imagination is increased. But I apprehend that all this is but guiding the imagination, freeing it from the dominion of the senses and passions, and placing it under its true lawgiver, — the idea of beauty; and that it does not increase its natural energy, which is always a gift of Nature. The decision does not lie with us whether there shall be imagination or not; or what degree of it there shall be. It exists equally energetic, whether cultivated or not. It presides over the sports of childhood just in the same ratio as that of the spirit to the body of the child. It acts in every walk of the most prosaic business. The victims of uncultivated imagination are all around us, — in the wild speculators of commercial life; in the insane pursuers of outward goods, to the destruction of all inward peace; in the fanatics of all sects of religion, and all parties of politics, and all associations for general objects. Nothing is to be gained by neglecting to use this faculty, or by omitting to give name to its movements, or by checking the soul's natural tendency to gratify it. Could we succeed in doing this, yet events would wake it up from its slumber, and might do so at any time; and it will be all the more liable to deem itself some god or demon from the hidden world, because it does not understand itself. To cultivate the imagination is rather to disarm its energy than to increase it; but in lieu of mere energy, cultivation gives beauty, safety, and elevating influences to all its movements.

But Mr. Alcott has no intention of cultivating one faculty more than another. His plan is to follow the natural order of the mind. He begins with analyzing the speech the children use. In doing this, they are led immediately to consider the action of the imagination, since it is this faculty which has formed language. We find that language clothes thoughts and emotions with the forms of nature, — its staple being the imagery of outward nature, as truly as the staple of sculptures and paintings is the material of outward nature, and all are Psyche's drapery. Mr. Alcott asks a child questions, in order to turn his attention upon what passes within his own mind; and what the child says, when making this inward survey, will determine what faculties are most active in his nature, for the time being. Or, if his words must be taken with caution, — and it is true that they sometimes must, since some children learn words by rote so easily, — his inward state can be determined, by taking a wide range of reading and constantly observing what character of books interests him most strongly. He will like those books best which exercise the faculties and feelings that are already in agreeable activity; and these should be cherished and nurtured, in a full confidence that they will wake up in due time the other faculties of the soul. Mr. Alcott, by pursuing this course faithfully, has found that the imagination is the first faculty which comes forth, leading all the others in its train. He has therefore not failed to meet it, and give it food. If he were to give it other than the healthy food supplied by Nature, Providence, and that true Genius which embodies Nature and Providence in its creations; or if he were to allow it to degenerate into fancy, or phantasy, or stray from the Principle of Beauty, which is the law of the imagination, I should be the last to defend it. But, wisely fed and governed, the imagination need not be feared. It is the concentration of profound feeling, reason, and the perception of outward nature into one act of the mind, and prepares the soul for vigorous effort in all the various departments of its activity.

Cambridge: Press of John Wilson and Son.

www.ingramcontent.com/pod-product-compliance
Lightning Source LLC
LaVergne TN
LVHW010213110826
845151LV00004B/1074
* 9 7 8 1 4 2 5 5 2 8 2 5 6 *